LIBERATING THE ADULT WITHIN

Moving from Childish Responses to Authentic Adulthood

HELEN KRAMER

SIMON & SCHUSTER
New York London Toronto Sydney Tokyo Singapore

SIMON & SCHUSTER
Rockfeller Center
1230 Avenue of the Americas
New York, New York 10020

SIMON & SCHUSTER and colophon are registered trademarks
of Simon & Schuster Inc.

Designed by Irving Perkins Associates
Manufactured in the United States of America

10 9 8 7 6 5 4 3 2 1

Library of Congress Cataloging-in-Publication Data
Kramer, Helen.
    Liberating the adult within : moving from childish responses to
authentic adulthood / Helen Kramer.
        p.   cm.
    Includes index.
    1. Emotional maturity.   I. Title.
BF710.K72   1994
158—dc20   93-49040
                                                                CIP

ISBN: 0-671-87009-2

To my parents
who taught me how to experience
the joy of being an adult

Acknowledgments

This book is inspired by love, and I have had many wonderful teachers. My parents had a miraculous capacity to create a loving home filled with warmth and affection, laughter and adventure. By seeing me with special eyes, and letting me know how valuable I was, they enabled me to grow into an adulthood that has been constantly enriching. Along with my parents, I was blessed with an ongoing affirmation from my many relatives. And my sister, Paula, has shared my life as an invaluable friend. In adulthood, Paula and I have had the chance to know each other both as women and as colleagues.

My husband, Paul, has continued to surprise me with his great capacity for love and caring. He is my companion in the wonderful adventure called marriage, and with him I have discovered that trust and pleasure have no limits.

This new great adventure of writing a book has been a fresh learning experience and a great inspiration.

My editor, Marilyn Abraham, gave me the confidence to believe I had a gift to give to the world, and that the excitement I found in my work could be passed on to others by writing about it. Marilyn encouraged me, prodded me, advised me, and helped me to shape, refine, develop, and search. She and my agent, Jane Dystel, were my guides as I embarked upon this foreign territory of book publishing. Jane helped me experience the power of my ideas, and led me through the confusing process of selling them. I credit Marilyn and Jane with making this book a reality.

Catherine Whitney, my collaborator on this project, made it a pleasure. She always respected my work in a way that inspired trust, while encouraging me to expand my ideas and feel the freedom to be excited. She challenged me, supported me, and helped to make my ideas resonate.

I am also grateful for the confidence shown by my dear friends, who have become an extension of my family circle. In particular, I want to thank Marci Rosen, Anne Ruderman, Marc Jaffe, Paul Franklin, Nina Yankowitz, Barry Holden, Scott Kumit, Rob Barnett, Joyce Kramer, Pat Lazzari, Luiz Pereira, Abbe Heller, Judy Keller, Corine Furnari, Richard Ellis, Tracey Mitchell, Michelle Vallon, Susan Friedberg, and Dr. Ray Brown. Each of them has offered their own blend of loving support, and has helped to bring vitality and fun to my life.

My students and clients have enabled me to take a theory and infuse it with meaning. I feel lucky to have such rich partners.

Finally, I want to express gratitude to the children in my life—Lila, Josh, David, and Nina—who have allowed me to participate in their growing and becoming truly wonderful human beings. They have filled my heart with wonder, and have allowed me the profound pleasure of participating in their journeys toward adulthood. Their unique gifts constantly add to my life, bringing a special magic and humility.

Contents

PART I

EMOTIONAL DYSLEXIA: WHEN AUTHENTIC ADULTHOOD ELUDES YOU

CHAPTER 1

The Emotional Triggers That Short-Circuit You

- Are you the confident, worthy adult you always thought you would be, or does life often throw you for a loop?
- Do you get frustrated because you think you should have more control?
- Are you embarrassed or unhappy when you react in certain ways, but find you can't help yourself?

What if I were to tell you that the reason you often don't feel like a confident, happy adult is that you suffer from what I call emotional dyslexia? Your parents may have had it; your teachers may have had it. Chances are, even your therapist has had it. It is a physiological phenomenon that has reached epidemic proportions. Emotional dyslexia is the fundamental impediment to being a full-fledged grown-up. It's the reason you explode when you want to feel calm, are fearful when you'd rather be brave, or are frustrated instead of successful.

You're probably familiar with the concept of dyslexia as it applies to learning. Very simply, the brain misinterprets the external and internal stimuli it receives and doesn't process it properly. For example, a person with dyslexia might recognize a word, but write it backward. It's the same thing with emotional dyslexia. Information from the outside is short-circuited in your brain. It bypasses the cognitive part of the brain where thinking occurs, and you react without the benefit of thought.

Emotional dyslexia is the reason you may sometimes fly off the handle when you'd really like to be reasonable. It's the reason that you sometimes do just the opposite of what you think you should do. It's the reason that your relationships are often explosive instead of nurturing.

Although you have probably condemned yourself many times about your inability to be the kind of adult you want to be, or to have the fulfilling relationships you know you're capable of, I want you to understand that emotional dyslexia is not your fault. Nor is it the result of some fundamental flaw that years of therapy may or may not resolve. Emotional dyslexia is a learning disability—and almost everyone has it. It has gone undiagnosed for the same reason other kinds of dyslexia were unexplored until fairly recently. Our understanding of the brain's workings have been relatively unsophisticated, but we're finding out more each year. And one important area where scientists and I agree is that there is a "feeling" reflex that is comparable to intellectual dyslexia. It's real and it's correctable.

The following five case studies will give you a clear idea of how emotional dyslexia manifests itself in the interactions of people. You'll see that there's nothing particularly "bad" or self-destructive about any of them. Their intentions are good. But in each case, a short circuit in the brain leads them to behave in ways that defy their own good intentions.

FRANCINE'S JEALOUS RAGE

Francine had been looking forward to going to this party with her husband Kevin all week. She'd spent most of the day preparing for it: getting her hair done, having a manicure, and buying a stunning new outfit. But as she sipped her drink and watched Kevin talking to their neighbor Joyce across the room, she felt anger sizzling in the pit of her stomach. He seemed to be having an awfully good time. And why shouldn't he, Francine thought gloomily. Joyce was young and beautiful. A natural wit, she was fun to talk to. Of course, Kevin was going to relish her company. Francine wished he would stop laughing with Joyce and come over and join her. But he never even glanced in her direction.

The more time Kevin spent with Joyce, the more upset Francine became. Rationally, she knew her mounting fury was baseless. A calm voice in her head recited the facts: Kevin loved her; his enjoyment of Joyce's company wasn't threatening to their marriage; he was just having fun. But even though Kevin had never given her a reason to doubt him, Francine couldn't seem to control her hurt and anger. It was as though a jealous, crazed "other Francine" had taken over. Suddenly, she decided that enough was enough. She jumped up from the couch and strode over to Kevin.

"I want to go home," she announced sharply.

Kevin looked at her with surprise. "But it's only ten o'clock. Is something wrong?"

"No, nothing's wrong." She glared at him. "I just want to leave."

"Well, I don't," he said. "I'm enjoying myself."

"I can see that," she answered sharply.

Kevin excused himself from Joyce, and turned to speak quietly with Francine.

"What's the matter with you?" He looked genuinely puzzled.

Francine couldn't stop herself. She felt her face reddening, her eyes welling with tears. Her voice rising, she practically spit at him. "I'm going home. Why don't you leave with Joyce—you seem to prefer her company to mine."

She turned and stormed out of the room, leaving a hushed silence behind her.

As soon as Francine reached the driveway, she began to regret what she had done. Was she out of her mind? She felt like an idiot. As her fury dissipated, her face grew hot once again with humiliation. What was she thinking? She'd made a fool of herself in front of their friends, and she'd ruined a perfect evening with her husband, who would now be very angry. She leaned against the car and started to cry. Was she a masochist or hopelessly neurotic?

JAKE'S TANTRUM

Jake and Susan were driving north from the city to spend the weekend at their country house. They were both in good moods because it was the first time they'd had a chance to get away for weeks. Jake was a top surgeon at a large city hospital, with a schedule so demanding that their time alone had become precious. They drove along, talking happily about their plans for the weekend. Jake began to feel the pressures of the past weeks disappear as they made their way along country roads.

Suddenly, the traffic ahead of them began to slow, and then ground to a complete halt. Jake immediately felt the tension reappear. His mouth tightened into a grimace. "What the hell is going on?" he muttered.

"Probably an accident," Susan said casually.

"Oh, that's just great." Jake pounded his hand on the steering wheel.

"Honey, relax. I'm sure it's nothing serious," Susan said soothingly.

Jake didn't answer. He felt the blood throbbing in his temples—the beginning of a major headache. Didn't she get it? He was stressed beyond the breaking point—and now this! He unsnapped his seat belt and got out of the car, slamming the door behind him. As he paced back and forth, swearing and kicking the tires of his car, he was aware that other drivers were watching him, and he felt silly. Damn! Why did he have to let a traffic jam make him so crazy? He broke into a half trot until he spotted the problem, then trotted back. Sweating and out of breath, he got back into the car. "Can you believe it?" he said to Susan. "Some stupid lady's car broke down and she's sitting there in the middle of the road. We'll never get out of here. She's ruining our weekend."

"I'm sure she didn't do it on purpose," Susan said. "Why don't we put on some music and relax?"

"Oh, shut up," Jake yelled. He wanted her to agree with him—to be as indignant as he was. He didn't need her patronizing attitude. "I've been working my tail off for weeks, and now I'm supposed to just sit here and watch the weekend waste away. Music isn't going to help."

Even after the traffic started moving, Jake continued to boil with anger. He knew he should apologize to Susan, but the words stuck in his throat. She was obviously hurt by his behavior, and the tension between them remained palpable for the rest of the evening.

The next day, Jake finally apologized, admitting he had overreacted. "I can't understand what got into me. At the hospital, I'm Mr. Calm. But being stuck in traffic . . . I don't know. It just makes me crazy."

ELEANOR'S BINGE

Eleanor looked at the clock again and sighed. She was miserable. Greg had promised he'd call. He even said he might come over, but it was almost ten o'clock and the phone hadn't rung all evening. Impatient, she'd even tried to call him, but his machine picked up, and the sound of his cheerful recorded voice was like a slap in the face. He was out doing something with someone else, and she was home alone.

She'd felt good at the start of the evening—optimistic about this new relationship, the first she'd had in a long time. She had lost most of the extra weight she'd put on during the past two years, and when she looked in the mirror, she could actually see herself as an attractive woman. But now she wondered. As she sat and stared at the phone that refused to ring, it occurred to her that maybe she wasn't really looking that good, after all. Keeping her weight down was a constant struggle, and maybe Greg liked those pencil-thin women favored in all the fashion ads. Well, she'd never be that thin. And if that's what he really wanted, well, to hell with him!

The feelings of loneliness and rejection were so strong that Eleanor began thinking of ways to comfort herself. She immediately considered the chocolate cake, sitting untouched on the kitchen counter. She'd planned to serve it to Greg when he came over, because she knew it was his favorite. Well, he didn't deserve it. Who knew where he was—out having fun while she sat there alone. She strode to the kitchen and pulled the cake from its box.

Eleanor ate the cake in gulps, barely stopping to taste it. She couldn't believe how quickly it disappeared. She took a knife and cleaned the frosting from the sides of the box. When she finished, she found that she wasn't satisfied. She still didn't feel better. She opened the refrigerator and began to rapidly pull items from the shelves—cold pasta with sauce, some tuna salad, the last of the bread pudding she'd made for Greg last week. She ate until she was so full she felt sick. Finally, Eleanor collapsed into a chair and put her head down on the kitchen table. She began to sob hopelessly. She hated Greg for not calling. She hated herself for being such a pig. Maybe she deserved to be alone. She was a disgusting person.

KAREN'S LOVESICK TRAUMA

When Karen met Phillip, she liked him immediately, and he seemed to like her, too. He called and asked her out on a date, and she was thrilled. They went to dinner and ended up talking long into the night. Phillip was one of the most open men Karen had ever met. He confided in her about his last relationship, which had ended several months earlier when his girlfriend of three years had left him for another man.

Karen's heart went out to Phillip. He seemed so vulnerable. When he told her he wasn't ready for anything but a casual relationship, she understood he felt that way because he had been so hurt. She was determined to show him he could trust women again.

In the weeks that followed, Phillip and Karen went out several times, and Karen knew she was falling in love. But every time she tried to get closer to him, Phillip pulled back and reminded her he wasn't ready. She really appreciated his honesty, and this made her try even harder to be nurturing. She baked cookies and took them to his apartment. She sent cute notes and cards to him.

Sometimes, Karen could see that her gestures made Phillip a little uncomfortable. She wondered if she was being too pushy, and she thought about pulling back a bit and giving him the room he said he wanted. But every time she resolved not to call him or write a note, she found herself unable to resist. She felt compelled to let him know how she felt about him. She couldn't stop herself from trying to be close to him, even though she feared it might drive him away. She thought about him all the time, and wanted the relationship to work so much that she seemed to have no control over the way she behaved.

Finally, after three months, Phillip told her, "I like you very much. You're a truly wonderful woman. But I don't feel right about us. You want more of a relationship than I'm prepared to give right now. I'm really sorry, Karen, but I think we should stop seeing each other."

Later, Karen sobbed to a friend, "I drove him away, just like I always drive men away. Why don't I ever learn? What's wrong with me? It seems I always ruin every relationship I'm in."

Her friend defended her. "Don't blame yourself. Phillip is just another man who sends mixed messages. He doesn't want a regular girlfriend, but he doesn't want to be alone, either. He drew you into a relationship; then when you started to get too close, he withdrew."

Karen desperately wanted to believe it was Phillip's fault, but in her heart she knew Phillip wasn't the problem. She had to face the fact that she knew all along he wasn't interested in getting involved. His behavior had never changed—only hers had because she wanted the relationship so much. She didn't know why she had shut out the obvious signals. Was she going to spend her entire life pursuing unavailable men? It scared her that she had so little control.

PETER'S BLAME GAME

Peter's department had just lost a big account, and now he had to face his boss and tell him what had happened. He knew he was responsible. He'd screwed up, made a crucial mistake. This could destroy his future with the company. Head pounding and stomach churning, he entered his boss's office.

His boss was clearly distressed, but he was a reasonable man. "What was the problem?" he asked Peter. "Is something wrong? It's not like you to drop the ball."

Peter squirmed in his seat, feeling humiliated. His stomach was tied in knots. His boss was being very objective about it, very decent, really. Peter knew he should just explain what had happened so they could discuss it like two professionals. He would shoulder the blame, take responsibility, and get it over with. But he couldn't do it. The words refused to come out of his mouth.

"Those guys in the design department didn't follow my instructions," he said, finally, feeling foolish for shifting the blame. "I told my assistant to double-check, but I guess he didn't."

Peter's boss didn't press him for further details, but Peter left his office feeling sick. Why had he behaved in this manner? He'd screwed up, and instead of admitting it, he'd pointed a finger in every direction but his own. He hadn't needed to. His boss wasn't threatening him. He didn't understand it himself. It was almost as if someone else had taken over his vocal chords and forced the words of blame from his mouth. Now he felt worse. Not only had he lost the account, he'd behaved like a whiny kid.

Do you see yourself, your friends, your coworkers, your family in any of these examples? Are you a veteran of therapy, self-help, or Twelve-Step programs, but are still not reaching your goals or maintaining the progress you've made? Does it sometimes seem you are being self destructive—as though you are your own worst enemy?

This is the complaint I hear most often when people come to my office. There seems to be no other reason why intelligent, capable people are making messes of their lives. People are filled with despair when they find themselves behaving just the opposite from how they want to behave. They're ashamed and embarrassed when they overreact or get too pushy or fail to take responsibility for their actions.

When people have spent years in therapy or self-help groups, they are particularly discouraged. They wonder if they're too far gone for help. They often speak of how ashamed they are that, regardless of the duration of their therapy, they are no closer to conquering the negative impulses that cause them so much trouble in daily life. Often, they describe themselves as generally well-functioning people who just seem to lose it in certain situations. Something will happen—a traffic tie-up, a misunderstanding, a canceled date, a confrontation at work—and they can't control their reactions. In my experience, people feel helpless. They want to be less anxious, hysterical, compulsive, or addictive, and they keep thinking, "I should stop." But they're propelled by the strength of their emotions.

I always feel great empathy when I hear that people can't help themselves, because I know it's the worst feeling in the world. The inability to behave like a thoughtful adult when things go wrong is so fundamentally demoralizing that it leaves people throwing up their hands and crying, "I'm messed up. I'm hopeless."

I don't believe that people are inherently bad or self-destructive, that they intentionally hurt others and shame themselves. Every client I've ever had, without exception, has wanted the same thing: to be happy and secure. And even when their actions appear destructive, most people have positive intentions. Consider the five people we met earlier in this chapter. Each of them reacted ineffectively when they were in a stressful situation. Yet they didn't do it because they wanted to make matters worse or cause a crisis. In each case, the intention was to achieve something good:

Francine loved her husband and wanted him to be enchanted with her instead of Joyce. She wanted to be sure they could maintain their loving closeness.

Jake wanted to get out of the traffic jam so he could enjoy a lovely weekend alone with Susan.

Eleanor wanted to have a relationship with Greg, because she liked him and she was lonely.

Karen wanted to experience the security and intimacy of
a romantic relationship.
Peter wanted to feel strong and competent at work.

These are all good intentions, based on the fundamental
human longing to be happy and feel that one's core being is
worthy. But in each case, when they sensed that a need wasn't
being met, they didn't know how to react effectively to a
stressful situation. And their responses caused disruptions,
unhappiness, and shame.

Francine, whose jealous rages were upsetting her married
life, explained it to me this way in a calmer moment: "I guess
I know why I feel jealous. I've always had trouble maintaining
long-term relationships with men. Kevin is the first one who
didn't find a reason to leave. So maybe deep down, I'm expecting it to happen—even though he hasn't given me any
reason. But I see that the more afraid I get that Kevin will
leave, the more I do things that drive him away."

Francine is a smart woman. She knows that jealousy hurts
her relationship. So, why doesn't she act upon what she
knows?

She thinks she has the answer: "Something is wrong
with me."

I disagree. What Francine is experiencing is the result of
emotional dyslexia. She wants one thing, but in the moment,
she gets the message in the wrong part of her brain. The part
that thinks—that can warn her that her emotions don't square
with reality—isn't operating when she needs it most.

THE CHILD/ADULT SPLIT

The easiest way to understand emotional dyslexia is to look at
the way the brain develops from the time we are infants.

During infancy, humans respond only to sensory input,

which triggers a reflexive response in the amygdala—the part of the brain where emotions exist. When a baby is hungry, hurt, or uncomfortable, he cries. He doesn't have a stored memory bank that tells him mom will come back.

As the neocortex or thought center of the brain develops in the young child, he begins to incorporate it to make distinctions. He doesn't necessarily cry when he is hungry, because the feelings of hunger don't cause panic. He knows that his parent will feed him. Likewise, if his mother leaves the house, he doesn't necessarily feel abandoned because he has a memory of other times she has done this and he realizes she'll be returning. He begins to use memory to help him cope with temporary losses. He becomes physically stronger.

With the maturation of the neocortex, human beings begin the journey toward adulthood. Ideally, adults would always respond in a well-rounded way, integrating their thoughts and emotions. So why are they so often consumed by the totally irrational responses of a young child?

The main thing that distinguishes a child from an adult is that a child really is dependent and helpless. He has very primitive resources to work things out on his own. If he reacts dramatically, it's understandable. Life truly is dramatic for him because he can't control himself or his environment.

I often refer to emotional dyslexia as being in the "child's state," because that is essentially what it looks and feels like. For example, children are often traumatized by change, since they lack the experience to know that change isn't necessarily dangerous. When adults react melodramatically to a change in their lives—falling in love, getting a new job, moving to an unfamiliar city—their brain is sending the same signals that a child receives.

But with adults, the reaction is different because they really *do* have more control. What happens with emotional dyslexia is that, when the adult is in a stressful situation, the emotional memory triggers childlike feelings, and the adult reacts accordingly. The neocortex is reduced to a helpless observer.

IT'S ORGANIC, NOT PSYCHOLOGICAL

My theory of emotional dyslexia is not psychological. Rather, it is an oganismic theory that cuts to the heart of how we live and the intrinsic nature of humans. Philosophically, it is based on the work of the American psychoanalyst Erik Erikson and the German neuropsychiatrist Kurt Goldstein. Erikson challenged previous theories that human maturation was completed at the end of adolescence. He showed that life has stages, and learning continues through adulthood. Goldstein's theory was that the basic instinct of all living organisms is to move toward mastery, and that every organism strives to do that unless the environment is inadequate. Erikson's theory demonstrated what is possible for human development. Goldstein's theory showed how environmental inadequacies could impede it, and he didn't use a pathological model—that is, that human behavior results from negative impulses.

My theory of emotional dyslexia (E.D.) is based on the premise that human beings are fundamentally oriented toward mastery or self-actualization unless something impedes them. In the case of E.D., the impediment is that important messages are going to the wrong part of the brain.

Current scientific research by leading neurobiologists confirms that when people are under stress, the messages to the brain will sometimes not reach the neocortex, causing a reaction from the amygdala before people have a chance to apply their thinking skills to the situation. In other words, you react without any help from your thinking brain. Until now, it was commonly assumed that your thoughts triggered your emotions. But my observations and new scientific evidence show that sensory input can go directly to your emotional centers.

According to Dr. Joseph Ledoux, of the Center for Neuroscience at New York University, who has conducted extensive studies of brain activity, "Emotional reactions and emotional memories can be formed without any conscious, cognitive participation at all, because anatomically the emotional system can act independently."

Ledoux explains that in humans this arrangement was meant to be in place only for life-and-death situations. In primitive times, when quick, instinctive reactions to danger could be lifesaving, this brain system was the primary means of protection. Even today, when people are in real danger, we often see them acting with exceptional power and speed.

Here is the problem: Although it is rare for people to encounter real life-or-death situations, they can't always make the distinctions that tell them this. They perceive danger where it doesn't necessarily exist, and the protective mechanism of the brain acts accordingly. For example, when Peter's boss confronted him, Peter's brain was flooded with fear before he even had a chance to evaluate the situation and formulate an appropriate response. He reacted automatically, as though he were in danger. He tried to protect himself when he didn't have to. Later, when he had a chance to think about what he'd done, he felt humiliated. It didn't make sense to him that he had behaved that way.

Emotional dyslexia most often occurs when it is triggered by stress. As Ledoux explains it, "Infantile emotional memories and adult fears and phobias can lie dormant (unconscious and unexpressed) for years until reinstated by stress." Something happens externally that throws you off balance, and you lose the ability to think. You just react. It doesn't matter if your emotional response is completely out of sync with the objective circumstances. Your brain literally does not hear the message from the neocortex.

TRANSFORMING EMOTIONAL DYSLEXIA

We live in a society where millions of people are in therapy, where billions of dollars are expended in the pursuit of happiness and personal power.

And yet, we look around and we don't see happy people. We don't see men and women living balanced lives. We don't see people finding satisfaction in their relationships. We don't see people comfortable with their bodies, or with the natural process of aging. Most people are overly stressed and they feel that they don't have enough control in their lives.

I began to address the problem of emotional dyslexia after I noticed a recurring pattern among the people who came to me for help. They had usually been working on personal growth issues for some time, and often good things had resulted. Maybe they had learned to feel less shame and to accept themselves. Or they had learned to express themselves more openly. But these were only partial solutions. Despite the fact that these men and women were very strongly motivated to change (they weren't enjoying being anxious, addicted, melodramatic, or "neurotic"), something was standing in the way.

It seemed logical to ask: If people were so committed to feeling better and making their lives work, why wasn't it happening?

I realized that something essential was missing from conventional therapy because so many people were experiencing the identical problem when they were under a lot of stress or faced new life issues. It isn't that therapy was wasted or even misdirected. But it had stopped short of giving them full power as adults.

I reached the conclusion that another kind of work was needed that wasn't therapy. Rather, what was needed was a reeducation—a way to train people in new patterns of response when their buttons got pushed, a training that helped people "grow up" their feelings so that their emotions re-flected their competence and maturity instead of letting un-controlled reactions create unwanted results.

If you examine most conventional and popular therapies, you'll notice that they are primarily focused on finding the root of the problem—be it a trauma in childhood or a dys-functional family dynamic that caused a blow to the ego. At first, it feels good when people discover that there are real causes for their problems. But knowing the cause isn't enough. Most psychologically oriented therapies don't take the next step of giving people lasting skills that will help them be more effective when they confront new problems. What may look like regression, resistance, masochism, and so on, may actually be explained by the recent discovery that emo-tional memories are indelible and will be triggered forever. Therapy isn't enough to transform the memories. Inevitably, people find that their ongoing failure to cope erodes the very foundation of their newfound "therapeutic" self-esteem. They reason that if they can't get better now that they know the cause of their problems, it must be their fault. They think they just didn't "get it," or were not really committed to changing, or they didn't work hard enough.

I believe the sick model is invalid. Think about it: Not everyone is hopelessly neurotic or self-destructive. Yet, even the most competent adults experience times when they can't seem to stop themselves from behaving like children.

One reason is simple: Nobody is perfectly balanced all of the time. It's a fact of human life. But I also believe the answer rests in the evolutionary immaturity of the human brain. There's no question that the brain is a wonder, and in some areas it has achieved remarkable feats. We can fly to the moon, invent miraculous technology, plan, organize, and make de-cisions—all the things that lower animals can't do. But these same abilities don't come into play when certain emotional buttons are pressed. A man may return from a successful business trip and have a big fight with his wife. A doctor may perform a brilliant operation, but still feel inadequate because her boyfriend breaks a date.

Most people have at least one area in their lives where they really feel out of control—where their reactions are getting in the way of happiness or success. Emotional dyslexia isn't limited to those who were raised in so-called dysfunctional families. Indeed, most of the people I see are not basket cases. But certain kinds of stresses trigger their precognitive emotions of insecurity, helplessness, and fear, and they can't control the way they react, because the memories—not of situations but of the emotional responses—from childhood are too strong. Remember the doctor, Jake? He realized there was something a little ridiculous about a brilliant surgeon kicking his car and hollering like a baby because he was stuck in a traffic jam. But the stress of being out of control was too great for him. It triggered a reaction in him that was similar to a child's.

LEARNING TO GROW UP

It's scary when you feel yourself being swept up in an emotional whirlwind that you know will only create greater problems. It's especially painful when your reactions come in an area of your life that you care about deeply. For example, you may desperately want to have a relationship, but every time you get involved with someone, you become petty, jealous, and overemotional. Or you want to lose weight, but you overeat when you get nervous and upset. Or you promise yourself that you won't yell at your child, but when he spills paint on your carpet, you explode.

The real pressures and anxieties of adulthood have you

stumped. So, what's the solution? How do you move away from the child's fearful reactions? How do you turn your positive intentions into reality? The simple answer is: You learn "smart" emotions.

There is no mystery to being a happy, successful adult. Your problem isn't that you're "sick"; it's that you haven't learned specific strategies for overcoming emotional dyslexia. Let's go back to the example of learning to read. If you were to place a book in front of someone who can't read, would you expect that person to identify the words? If he couldn't, would you say, "You're a bad person. What's wrong with you?" Of course not. You'd say, "You need to be taught to read." It's the same with adult skills. If certain situations cause you to respond like a frightened child, it's because you haven't learned the adult replacement response.

I've developed strategies to deal with emotional dyslexia that begin with the premise that people are not bad, masochistic, or neurotic. In twenty years of work, I have never met anyone who wanted to suffer or who wasn't eager to move toward happiness, if shown how. When I teach people replacement behavior, they discover power where they didn't believe it existed. They're euphoric when they realize they're not sick, just unskilled. "I swear, I thought I had a genetic defect that made me hopelessly inept at being in love," a woman told me, suddenly relieved of the humiliating label of being obsessive. "Now I see that I can do this."

Let's consider Karen's reaction, earlier in this chapter, when she began to fall in love with Phillip. Falling in love is very stressful, and in Karen's case, it filled her with fear. She longed to fall in love so badly that she became overly possessive, even though a persistent voice inside told her that she was driving him away. She couldn't change her intense childlike emotions because she had never learned to act in any other way when she was interested in a man. She lacked the skills that would have helped her evaluate the situation and respond differently.

In the same way you learned other adult skills, like driving a car, using a computer, or cooking a meal, you can learn to engage your thinking brain before you react to stress.

Time and again, I find that when I teach people smart emotions to replace childish responses, they are able to transform their lives. It is remarkable to see the tremendous release that occurs when they realize they are neither out of control nor perpetual victims of their emotions. Given the chance, people are eager and willing to do what they can to overcome the barriers to their happiness.

Let's Learn Together

Emotional dyslexia is the most common reason for the pain, anxiety, and unhappiness that afflict our daily lives. If you are suffering, know that you need not continue to do so. I invite you to learn a different way of using your brain that will change your life. It's not a simplistic solution. It's not magical. But I assure you that learning is possible.

Join me in investigating your potential to be a fully functional, secure adult. In the pages of this book, you will meet many people who have problems and stresses similar to yours. Like you, they want to make their lives work and to stop acting in ways that prevent happiness. You'll find that they are good, worthy people, just as you are. They simply haven't been exposed to the skills that will allow them to transform their behaviors.

In the next chapter, I will introduce you to the foundation of my work—the Emotional Dyslexia Index. It will serve as the basic tool in your education process. Once I teach you smart emotions, you'll find they come naturally, like learning good nutrition. I ask you to work with me and determine for yourself if my approach makes sense. Walk through the process with me. Experiment with the E.D. Index and see if you start to feel better. I believe these tools can help you function more ably in the very areas where you had given up hope of changing.

CHAPTER 2

The E.D. Index: Rewire Your Hot Buttons

The E.D. Index is a detection method that alerts you when you're slipping into a child's state and a guidance system that offers you the appropriate adult response in its place. It will help you gain adult mastery in every situation. Simply, in times of crisis and vulnerability, it stops you short and issues a warning: *Don't trust your reactions now. Don't make decisions when you're feeling this way. Don't act while you're in this state.* It will then give you an alternative response that comes from an adult perspective, which is: *Stop. Think. Review.*

You can learn to be released from emotional dyslexia and retrained to use your smart emotions in stressful situations. Over time, as you internalize the E.D. Index, you'll more quickly recognize certain knee-jerk reactions, such as shame, impatience, and jealousy, as being the child's way of reacting. And you'll be able to flip the switch into an adult response. The adult replacement emotions reflect the integration of your emotions and your intellect.

I'm giving you this tool because it has been my experience that it's not enough to know something is wrong. It doesn't help you just to be told that you have emotional dyslexia—as though it were a new dysfunction to add to all the others. You also need a method for transforming the problem. My view is

ᴇd by Dr. Ledoux, who believes that emotional mem-
 so tenacious that they cannot be erased; they must be
transformed. Ledoux theorizes that, "Treatments that empha-
size cortical control may prove to be more effective . . . than
those that attempt to eliminate indelible and cognitively im-
penetrable emotional associations." People can live more fully
and competently when they learn new emotional responses,
or "smart emotions."

As you review the E.D. Index, keep in mind that it's not
a static model. The reactions of the child or adult states may
occur simultaneously. In fact, if you're exhibiting one child
state, it's likely that you're experiencing others, too. The same
holds true for the reactions of adult states. The format of the
E.D. Index is designed to demonstrate the many facets of
these states, so you'll have an easier time recognizing them
when they occur.

The E.D. Index gives you a vivid portrait of what it feels
like to be in a child or adult state. It's the beginning of emotional learning—the process that will help you bypass your
emotional dyslexia.

THE E.D. INDEX
A GUIDE TO ADULT/CHILD RESPONSES

ADULT	CHILD
Interdependency	*Dependency*
Worthiness	Shame
Freedom	Victimization
Power	Impotence
Awareness	*Distortion*
Empathy	Egocentricity
Patience	Impatience
Reality	Fantasy

Confidence	*Fear*
Flexibility	Rigidity
Fulfillment	Jealousy
Peace	Melodrama

Interdependency, awareness, and confidence are the primary adult states. Dependency, distortion, and fear are the primary child states. Within each state are three typical ways of reacting. These provide the tangible clues that you're responding to a situation from either an adult or child state. The following is a description of the feelings you have—and the accompanying internal dialogue—when you're experiencing any of these reactions.

ADULT STATE	CHILD STATE
Interdependency	*Dependency*
WORTHINESS	**SHAME**
"Everyone makes mistakes."	"What's wrong with me?"
• You have a sense of humor about life's imperfections.	• You're obsessed with appearing to be perfect.
• You know it's okay to have needs.	• You think you have to hide your needs.
• You expect to make mistakes, and expect others to make them, too.	• You feel humiliated when things go wrong.
FREEDOM	**VICTIMIZATION**
"I can get what I need."	"I have bad karma."
• You can act interdependently and still achieve intimacy.	• You seek symbiosis with others.
• You expect life to contain pain, so it doesn't overwhelm you.	• When you experience pain, you feel like you're being singled out for punishment.

- You're not afraid of being abandoned.

POWER

"I do make a difference."

- You're not threatened by change, separation, and conflict.
- You can accept responsibility for the consequences of your actions.
- You know how to make a difference.

- You're terrified of being alone.

IMPOTENCE

"Nothing I do matters."

- You can't feel good unless your relationships are harmonious.
- You don't accept responsibility for what happens.

- You feel unable to affect the course of events.

ADULT STATE	CHILD STATE
Awareness	*Distortion*

EMPATHY

"Sometimes things happen that we can't control, even when we have the best intentions."

- You see somebody else's point of view as separate from your own.
- You can relate to the needs of others without fearing that your own needs won't be met.
- You can observe and respond with a sense of fullness.

PATIENCE

"This feels lousy, but it will pass."

- You keep in mind the past and the future.

EGOCENTRICITY

"How can you do this to me?"

- You can't see somebody else's point of view.
- You see your own intense needs as the only needs.

- You personalize everything that happens.

IMPATIENCE

"I can't stand this feeling."

- You lack memory of the past or perspective on the future.

- You don't let isolated disappointments spoil everything.

- You avoid making snap judgments.

REALITY

"My life isn't perfect, but I have much to be thankful for."

- You know it takes effort to solve problems.
- You look at the entire context, not just isolated incidents.
- You accept bad news, even when it is painful.

- You demand instant gratification and you can't tolerate ambiguity.
- You have to act immediately and force resolutions prematurely.

FANTASY

"Everything is supposed to be perfect."

- You believe in magical solutions to problems.
- You don't understand the context so you invent explanations that are unrealistic.
- You refuse to hear, see, or remember reality because it's too difficult to accept.

ADULT STATE	CHILD STATE

Confidence

FLEXIBILITY

"What are the options?"

- You know that life is complex.
- You can create options for handling problems.
- You can tolerate ambiguity without getting anxious.

Fear

RIGIDITY

"My way or the highway."

- You see everything as black and white.
- You need rules and absolutes to function.
- You're easily overwhelmed when you don't have all the answers.

FULFILLMENT

"I know I have limitations, but I'm happy with who I am."

- You're not diminished by the good fortune of others.

JEALOUSY

"He (she) has all the luck."

- You don't think there are enough good things to go around

- You find pleasure in the world as it is.
- You look inward, instead of comparing yourself to others.

PEACE

"I can handle my life."

- You appreciate the ironies and unpredictabilities of life.
- You understand the difference between feeling discomfort and being in danger.
- You know that life can be lived fully in spite of deferred dreams and personal disappointments.

- You judge yourself in comparison to others.
- You envy others and feel diminished by their success.

MELODRAMA

"I can't live like this!"

- You see life as unpredictable and dangerous.
- You can't distinguish between real and imagined danger.
- You're overly upset when things don't go your way.

THE E.D. INDEX IN REAL LIFE

Remember the five people I introduced in the first chapter? Francine, Jake, Eleanor, Karen, and Peter all found that emotional dyslexia interfered with the positive results they wanted. How might they have responded differently and more effectively, under the circumstances?

By using the E.D. Index to examine the internal dialogue that was playing when they reacted childishly, we can develop a different internal dialogue that might have given them more perspective. In every case, the adult's internal dialogue is quite different from the child's, and it leads to an entirely different behavior. The child's dialogue, motivated by dependency, distortion, and fear, paralyzes, upsets, and inevitably makes things worse. The adult's dialogue, emanating from a desire for interdependency, awareness, and confidence, transforms the situation and allows positive action.

Francine, who erupted in a jealous rage because her husband was spending too much time at the party talking to their neighbor, behaved like a jealous, humiliated child. She would have responded differently if she had been able to recognize that jealousy was a precognitive emotion and would have replaced it with an adult response. Here's a comparison of the two internal dialogues, using the E.D. Index:

Dependency

"If Kevin is going to spend so much time talking to Joyce, I'm going to have a terrible time at this party. People at the party are going to see how much Kevin and Joyce enjoy each other, and they're going to think he's more interested in her than in me because she's so young and beautiful and full of life."

Interdependency

"There are friends here that I've been dying to talk to. I don't need to sit here watching Kevin and Joyce. Kevin and Joyce are doing what friends do—they're having a good time. I'm not as beautiful as Joyce, but I like who I am, and so does Kevin."

Distortion

"He doesn't care about me. He'd rather be with Joyce. I want him to come over here and be with me now."

Awareness

"Kevin has been a loving husband for twelve years. I don't need him to pay attention to me every minute to prove he loves me."

Fear

"Joyce is so young and thin. Of course, Kevin would prefer to spend time with her. What if he decides he wants her more than he wants me?"

Confidence

"Joyce looks fantastic. I wish I could be in such great shape. But never mind. I know I look pretty terrific tonight, and Kevin said he loved this new dress on me. Besides, Kevin has lots of women friends, and I have lots of male friends. We're both very sociable people, and that's one of the things we always enjoyed about each other."

Jake, who blew up when he got caught in traffic, might have replaced his irrational precognitive emotions with an adult response, if he'd known how to view the situation in another way. Here's the difference, using the E.D. Index:

Dependency

"Susan always has to be so calm and together. She's so perfect—she makes me feel like a jerk."

Interdependency

"Susan is wonderful to try and soothe me. She knows how hard I've been working and how irritated I get in traffic jams. It makes me feel good to know she's here."

Distortion

"Why do I have to get stuck in traffic, after the lousy week I've had? It's not fair. I can't stand it when other people screw up. That woman is ruining our weekend."

Awareness

"If I have to be stuck in a traffic jam, at least I'm in good company. These things happen. That woman didn't want her car to break down. Besides, it's frustrating for Susan, too. Anyway, we'll lose an hour, but it's no big deal. We'll get there eventually, and then we'll have the whole weekend to relax. Traffic jams don't last forever."

Fear

"My weekend is ruined. I'll never be able to unwind."

Confidence

"Traffic jams are common, especially on weekends. I don't have to let it ruin my mood. I can listen to music or talk to Susan. It won't seem so important later when we're relaxing on our deck."

Eleanor binged on cake because she felt lonely and rejected when Greg failed to call her as he had promised he would do. To punish him, and to try to soothe herself, she ate the cake she had bought to please him. A further child's response told her she was disgusting for eating the cake, and this compelled her to eat even more, discarding any semblance of control. Once her child's reaction got going, she couldn't stop it. Using the E.D. Index, we can see how she might have responded differently had she been able to view the situation from an adult perspective.

Dependency

"He's out having a good time while I'm here alone and miserable. And no wonder he doesn't want to be with me. I'm a pig."

Interdependency

"I don't like waiting for a call that doesn't come. I don't know Greg well enough to know if there's a problem or if he's just irresponsible. I know I didn't do anything wrong."

Distortion

"I can't stand not knowing why Greg didn't call. I feel so awful, I have to do something right now to make me feel better."

Awareness

"The cake only tastes good in the beginning. But I'll be miserable if I eat too much. Besides, I don't really want cake. I want Greg."

Fear

"How can I have a relationship with a man? I can't even control my eating. Why do men always make me feel out of control?"

Confidence

"I can help myself. I can control my urge to overeat and see that overdosing on food doesn't really make me feel better. And if I'm lonely, I can call my friend Gail. She'll make me laugh."

When Phillip broke up with Karen, she felt the same hopelessness and self-defeat she had felt when other relationships failed to work out. Using the E.D. Index, we can see how she might have approached the situation in a different way:

Dependency

"There I go again, ruining a perfectly good relationship. I'm too pushy. If I hadn't been so needy, he wouldn't have ended things."

Interdependency

"Phillip isn't withdrawing because of me. He has his own issues to deal with. This was the wrong time for him, that's all."

Distortion

"I was only trying to show him how supportive I can be. If I just keep it up, I'm sure he'll come around."

Awareness

"I hear Phillip saying that he needs some space right now. Even though he likes me, he has issues that have nothing to do with me. I guess I understand how he's feeling. After my last breakup, I went into hiding and wanted nothing to do with men for a long time."

Fear

"I've been alone so long, and it's felt so bad. I can't stand the thought of losing him and being alone again. What if I never meet another nice guy? What if I never fall in love again?"

Confidence

"I'm really sorry. I liked Phillip so much. But he isn't the only good man on earth. I'll still have other opportunities."

Peter's mistake at work, and the embarrassment it caused him, drove him into the child because he was afraid of looking foolish. Using the E.D. Index, we can see how he might have looked at the situation another way:

Dependency

"I can't believe I let this account get away. Maybe I'm not so good, after all. The boss is going to blame me for everything."

Interdependency

"I know I'm good at my job. This mistake was major, but mistakes happen. I can't believe I let this one get away from me, but even the best in the business screw up sometimes. I need to get a handle on what happened so it doesn't happen again."

Distortion

"I'll be ruined. One mistake is all it takes to destroy years of good work."

Awareness

"I've been working at this company for six years, and everyone says I've done a great job. One mistake doesn't cancel out six years. I didn't suddenly go from being good at my job to being bad at my job."

Fear

"If I don't find some way to get out of this mess, I'll look like a jerk, and maybe lose my promotion."

Confidence

"I can accept responsibility with dignity. It will make me feel more confident, and pay off in the long run."

The adult responses might seem pat, and you may read them skeptically, thinking, "Who could ever remain so calm and reasonable?" Well, no one stays perfectly balanced all of the time. The adult responses I've given are not the exact words someone is thinking or saying. Rather, the viewpoints expressed are reflective of the general state of adulthood. Until you get used to replacing the familiar old child responses with their adult counterparts, they'll sound awkward. But consider this: If you go back and examine each situation, you can see in every case how the child's reactive behavior obscured the truth of the situation.

Francine's husband was not going to leave her for Joyce. Jake wasn't going to be stuck in traffic all weekend. Eating the cake wasn't going to make Eleanor feel better. Karen wasn't going to make Phillip love her by ignoring his warning that he wasn't ready for a serious relationship. Peter wasn't going to feel more competent because he blamed his coworkers for his mistake. As long as the child's precognitive emotions are allowed to lead and motivate, no problem gets solved—and people feel worse in the bargain.

How to Learn Adult Skills

The E.D. Index is a blueprint for a successful pattern of adult behavior. It will provide the foundation upon which you can begin to develop a new way of responding to the complexities of being and behaving like a grown-up.

Each of the following chapters focuses on a common E.D. trigger—a stress that tends to drive people into a child state. Each chapter is followed by a lesson, which will teach you a specific adult skill. These skills are the cornerstone to living and relating as an adult. They will teach you to:

- Discover your adultness
- Achieve intimacy without losing your power
- Remember your worth when you're feeling low
- Accept differences without judging
- Forgive your parents for their past mistakes
- Be an adult with your children
- Find your power when it seems you have none

Like any learning process, this one takes practice. I'll show you many ways adult responses can be observed, practiced, and applied in real life situations, and give you some practical lessons you can do on your own or with others. I've found that there are many different ways people learn: by reading, by talking with others, by noticing things for the first time from a different perspective. But emotional learning always occurs in the world, not in a closet. Your most effective learning will happen as you practice adult responses in the ordinary course of your days—and as you notice the responses of others. The lessons merely serve as a guide to point you in the right direction. They're designed to help you become a better observer of your own reactions and those of others—to step outside the familiar pattern of childlike responses and screen things through your adult brain.

I encourage you to practice them with your friends and family—to engage in others in the learning process. It might seem hard at first, but you don't have to do it alone. In the beginning, I'm going to do the work for you—to lead and teach you. That's because it's impossible to change behavior unless you have a replacement. Learning doesn't happen in a vacuum. I'm going to guide you: "Instead of X, try Y." If you think that your current ineffective responses are just "doing what comes naturally," I'll teach you a new "natural" way to respond.

I promise you that with time, choosing an adult response will become easier. I have found through extensive work with individuals and groups that emotional learning ultimately changes the response reflex for good. Over time, your learned response will become the one that is automatic. You'll experience a physiological shift—much like a muscle responds differently when it is exercised repeatedly. Finally, most of the time your reflexive reaction will be the adult's, not the child's, response.

You'll find that it's great being an adult. You'll be more spontaneous and energetic. You'll feel more creative because you'll be able to use your full store of adult experiences, without being constrained by the child's limitations.

Whenever I work with people and teach them adult responses, they become more alive and vital. They gain a sense of humor about life that they didn't have before. They feel more attractive and interesting because they no longer judge themselves in the rigid, one-dimensional scope of a child.

It's hard to be a child in an adult world, because you haven't got any control. It's exhausting to be tormented by emotional trauma, to be paralyzed by fear, to feel helpless to achieve the things that matter most to you. I assure you, it's much better—and easier!—to be an adult.

PART II

ADULT SOLUTIONS TO
LIFE'S BIG QUESTIONS

CHAPTER 3

Can You Make Your Relationships Work?

- **Do you feel like you have a self-destruct button when it comes to relationships?**
- **Are you confused about what's realistic to expect from friends and lovers?**
- **Are your relationships filled with anxiety and drama?**

Where does emotional dyslexia most often show up? In relationships with those who are nearest and dearest to our hearts. Love—be it romantic or friendship—pushes our child buttons like nothing else. Precisely because love is the source of our greatest gratification, it can also generate the greatest emotional uproar.

This story may sound familiar to you. Elaine was distraught over a bitter fight she'd had the night before with Mark, the man she was dating. "I blew up at him and I shouldn't have, but I can't take it back, and now he isn't speaking to me," she said miserably.

Elaine had told me many times how happy she was to have found Mark. But I knew she thought their relationship was still very fragile. I asked her to tell me what had happened.

"We had a date to see a play," she said. "We'd both been looking forward to it. But the day before, Mark called and said he couldn't make it. He's a freelance photographer and a job came up. I can't explain why, but something in me snapped. I hit the roof and said all kinds of angry things. You know the list: 'How could you do this to me?' 'Don't you care about me?'—that kind of thing. Mark stayed really calm for a while, but I just couldn't let it go. Finally, he got mad, then I slammed down the phone, and we haven't talked since." She sighed. "Helen, I blew it with the first man I've cared about in a long time. I acted like a shrew. Mark's a great guy, and this morning, in the light of day, I realized I was totally out of line. But why do I do things like this? I feel like I have a self-destruct button when it comes to relationships, and I pushed it. I just can't believe it. You'd think that after seven years of various kinds of therapy, I'd have more control."

But Elaine's response to Mark wasn't about lack of control. Nor did she have a self-destruct button when it came to men—something that she, like many women, believed about herself.

Elaine was merely experiencing a familiar fear that went something like this:

Being loved feels good.

Therefore, I want to be loved. When I am being loved, I feel happy.

If it seems like I'm not being loved (or risk not being loved in the future), my happiness is jeopardized, and I become scared.

When I'm scared, I either become self-critical or I lash out at the person who is the source of my distress.

The fear of being unloved can seep into all important relationships—be they with a lover, a spouse, or a close friend.

Conventional therapy provides some relief, but, time and again, I see people like Elaine who can't understand why these dramatic posttherapy lapses occur. The more they care about a relationship working, the less capable they are of making it happen.

Before she started therapy, Elaine was "looking for love in all the wrong places"—consistently involved in relationships that ended badly—a painful affair with a married man, a lover who was an abusive alcoholic, and another lover who was so critical that she felt like her nerves were on edge every moment. Each one of these relationships left her feeling increasingly undesirable.

Therapy helped Elaine discover a feeling of self-worth she had never had before, and provided her with the validation that was missing from the men in her life. She began to believe that she was okay whether a particular man thought so or not. This new self-esteem gave Elaine the courage to pursue relationships with more stable men. When she met Mark, a nice man who seemed to genuinely like her, she was pleased and proud that she was finally on a positive track. Now, as she recalled her behavior when Mark broke their date, she couldn't believe that she might have thrown all those years of work away on a single temper tantrum. "I'm back to square one," she moaned.

I felt Elaine's anguish, but her story was not unfamiliar to me. One of the myths of therapy is that people grow along a linear line. They "gain" self-esteem or wisdom and expect to hold onto it forever. But life is more complex than that, and the good feelings that sometimes come from therapy are only half the battle. *Knowing* you're good is one thing; learning how to *apply* that sense of goodness, especially in the midst of a crisis, is far more challenging. Elaine's therapy wasn't wasted—nor was she backtracking. She was just discovering the place where therapy was incomplete.

Elaine's upset with Mark was not based on a real threat, but his call stimulated her precognitive emotions. Once she was set off, she couldn't calm herself down because the feelings were so strong and so familiar. They seemed so real.

This is a big problem for many people. The intense feelings that are stimulated automatically by stressful occurrences feel so real that people react without questioning the validity of their feelings. The sense that, "If I feel it, it must be real, and I must act upon it," is one sign of emotional dyslexia. But many people, like Elaine, find that when they express strong feelings, it often provokes the opposite of what they desire. That's because the feelings themselves were an emotionally dyslexic response. They were keenly felt, but they weren't valid.

THE STRESS OF LOVING

All of your close relationships will feel overly stressful if the only thing you have to help you are a child's tools for coping. Love is an affirmation of our goodness, so it is bound up with our selfhood and expectations for happiness, that it becomes very easy to let the child take over. Add to that the fact that you learned virtually everything you know about relationships when you were very young—before you had cognitive skills to help you. Your parents, well meaning as they might have been, probably didn't have the ability to teach you different skills as you matured. So you've been stuck in a child's way of relating to the people you care about. If you review the E.D. Index, you might hear some familiar reactions from the child's side:

1. *Dependency.* Because you like being with the other person, you can feel too needy. Especially in the beginning of a relationship, it can seem as though the other

person's love is a lifeline that you must have. So you constantly adjust your behavior to please the other person.

2. *Distortion.* Since you believe that love happens by magic—either chemistry or fate—you lack a perspective on what makes a good relationship develop. You grow overly focused on each moment and have an extreme reaction if the person you love doesn't behave in a loving way all the time.

3. *Fear.* You're always worried that the relationship might fail, and you're constantly on the lookout for the signs. This fear is very stressful and it leads you to overreact to the slightest ripple of trouble. Everything about the relationship is blown out of proportion.

All of these states are manifestations of the child's emotional immaturity—and yet we see them played out again and again in adult lives. There are strong components of the child in every romantic movie or book, and we are bombarded with images every day that tell us how the ideal family should be, how to have perfect sex, or what to do to attract the man or woman of our dreams. In the fantasy world of television and movies, everyone seems surrounded by loyal, loving friends, a warm, supportive family, and passionate partners. It's nearly impossible to escape the cultural brainwashing that keeps us in a child's state of anxiety and helplessness.

THE CHILD CRAVES SYMBIOSIS

Adult relationships often trigger these reactions because most of us have a strong emotional memory of the core relationships of our childhood, when being close to another human being meant symbiosis. A baby is literally at one with his mother. Every conscious moment is tied to her presence—her voice, her smell, her feel, her appearance. The mother is synonymous with a child's well-being. As the infant matures, the symbiosis lessens and he becomes more independent, but the young child still craves constant emotional and physical closeness. And in a practical sense, he still depends on his mother to meet all of his needs. Toddlers can't fix their own food or dress themselves or go places alone. Their everyday lives revolve around what their mothers (or caretakers) do.

People confuse what early love can do and what later love can do. Subconsciously, many adults try to create perfect relationships and achieve the symbiotic love they needed but didn't get as infants. Indeed, an intimate adult moment can feel like symbiosis. You want to keep it forever, and it can be a jolt when you find that the loving feelings experienced only hours or moments ago can't be sustained all of the time.

I remember a friend describing a wonderful weekend she'd spent with her husband. It was one of those extended periods of warmth and intimacy when everything seemed just perfect. Her husband had been especially attentive and caring, and they returned home in a glow of good feelings. That evening, they were snuggling on the couch watching television. She went to change the channel and dropped the remote control.

He quickly picked it up and said, "I'll handle it."

She snapped, "Oh, shut up! You've been waiting all weekend for a chance to put me down." She jumped up and stormed out of the room.

All of the closeness of the past three days evaporated in an instant. She was focused on the moment, and in that moment her husband didn't sound loving. So, everything else they had experienced during the past three days was without merit.

This is an example of the painful outcomes of emotional dyslexia. People expect love relationships to be symbiotic, and when the harsh, human moments occur, they think there is something deeply wrong with the relationship.

The truth is, nobody but an infant needs (or gets) symbiosis. But because love makes people feel so good, and the intimacy that comes with it can seem so much like symbiosis, the emotionally dyslexic lover gets a chemical message from the brain demanding constant, uninterrupted closeness. When that closeness doesn't exist, even for a day or a moment, the reaction can be extreme. Suddenly, an entire relationship is threatened because of a single incident. The reaction is not unlike the way a baby reacts when you pull a pacifier from her mouth.

That is what happened to Elaine. When Mark broke their date, her message center went berserk and she reacted accordingly. Instead of being realistic about the circumstances (he broke the date because a job had come up), she distorted them. In that moment, everything she and Mark had experienced together was threatened. She was temporarily blinded to the plausible explanation that unpredictable events occur all the time. Adult life is full of unforeseeable situations. They are normal and usually not dangerous. Elaine responded as though her relationship with Mark was jeopardized. As we talked, I tried to help Elaine objectify her experience, and show her how adult skills might have allowed her to create a different result.

"Put aside what really happened when Mark called and told you he wasn't going to be able to make it," I suggested, "and let's take it from the beginning. You were disappointed that Mark canceled the date."

"To say the least," she groaned.

"I know, it felt like more than that. But wouldn't you say, now that you've had time to think about it, that your basic feeling was one of disappointment?"

"Yeah," she nodded. "I guess. It wasn't even the show I

cared about. I wanted to spend time with Mark. I was looking forward to it. I had the whole evening planned."

"There's nothing wrong with feeling disappointed when you've gone all out and your plans fall through," I assured Elaine. "That's a pretty normal emotion. The problem is, you couldn't find an adult way to express your upset. You were overwhelmed by your initial feelings of disappointment, and that tide carried you into the child's state, where you reacted melodramatically."

I asked Elaine to consider what might have happened if she had simply expressed her feelings of disappointment at the very start. I asked her to role-play in order to explore both her and Mark's reactions.

MARK: "I'm sorry. I can't make it. This job I've been waiting for came up, and I have to take it."

ELAINE: "Oh, I'm so disappointed. I was looking forward to this evening."

MARK: "Yeah, me too. Maybe we can exchange the tickets for one night next week."

ELAINE: "I doubt it. They're almost impossible to come by."

MARK: "I guess you're right. I'm sorry. I'll make it up to you this weekend. I just wanted to be with you, anyway. The play isn't important."

Elaine grew very quiet on the other end of the phone line. When she finally spoke, her voice was low and thoughtful. "I wish I could trade this conversation for the one we had. I actually felt good at the end of it, even though Mark was still breaking the date."

Indeed, by reacting in a melodramatic manner and giving herself over to the feelings of a fearful child, Elaine lost her power. The result of venting inappropriate feelings is that we often drive away the very people we are afraid will abandon us. Feelings only make sense in context. If Mark had said to Elaine, "I've changed my mind. I don't want to be with you," or made some other provocative statement, her anger might have been justified. If throughout their relationship, Mark had consistently broken dates, her response might have actually felt empowering—a way to stop submitting to his behavior. But that wasn't the case.

I've had people tell me that when they really care about a relationship, they're resigned to feeling out of control. As adults, we need to acknowledge this uncertainty while not letting it drive us into the child's state. Often people demand too much reassurance, call too much, take everything too personally—as though they're actually expecting the relationship to fall apart. They might even be aware that they're not helping, but they can't stop themselves. The result is that relationships often cause high anxiety and, ultimately, disappointment. It doesn't have to be that way. Because people have never had the experience of responding any other way, it feels inevitable. But adult skills are available to everyone— even someone who's in love.

FRIENDS CAN TRIGGER E.D. REACTIONS, TOO

It isn't just romantic relationships that push our buttons. I see the same dynamic occurring all the time in close friendships. People tend to have unrealistic expectations of the way friends should be, and they are frequently disappointed when reality doesn't measure up. Think of how you relate to your friends. Do any of these sentiments sound familiar?

Friends should **always** be there for you.
Friends should **always** be supportive, no matter what.
A true friend will **always** take your side.
A friend's presence is **always** welcome.

There's a recurring theme in these statements, contained in the word *always*. All close relationships can trigger E.D. because when we need closeness and we're not getting it, this will stimulate what it felt like as a child to not have a need met. Our early unmet needs, coupled with unrealized adult needs, can lead to a special intensity. We feel supported by our friendships; they are the visible evidence of our lovability. But like romantic relationships, friendships often fall victim to our fantasies of perfection.

Even if you don't agree with the statements above, can you honestly say that you've never been hurt when a friend didn't return a phone call, disagreed with you about something important, or failed to include you in a social event? At one time or another, most people have experienced the pain of feeling slighted by a friend. The story of Mary and Jean is a case in point.

When Jean told her best friend Mary that she was in love with Ron, Mary threw her arms around her in a warm embrace. "That's wonderful!" she cried. "I'm so happy for you."

Mary was genuinely pleased for her friend. She'd been with Jean through a long, stormy period following the breakup of her last relationship. She was glad that maybe Jean was going to find what she was looking for. She felt good when Jean told her, "None of this would have happened if I hadn't had a good friend like you to buck me up and keep me sane."

As the months went by, Jean's new relationship blossomed, and she excitedly told Mary that she and Ron were talking about marriage. Again, Mary was happy for Jean, but she was also feeling a little bit left out because Jean didn't have too much time for her anymore. She tried to be understanding about it. It was only natural that Jean would want to spend more time with Ron.

When Jean got engaged and began preparing for her wedding, she was busier than ever, and Mary's conversations with her were rushed and unsatisfying. As Mary's sense of isolation grew, she began to resent the way Jean so easily dropped their relationship. She understood that her friend was busy, but she hadn't expected the change to be so major. Mary thought she knew what was happening. Now that Jean had found her man, Mary wasn't that important to her anymore. Mary felt abandoned and jealous. Not only had she lost her best friend but she had no man in her life. Jean had it all, and she was left with nothing.

By the time Mary appeared in one of my workshops, she was feeling lousy. I could read her distress in the slump of her shoulders, but she admitted right away that she was being pulled between two emotions. "I find myself getting angry and resentful because Jean is too busy for me," she said. "Then I hate myself for being jealous. It's so confusing. How can you love someone and yet resent their happiness?"

Mary's dilemma was common. I had seen it many times. When a close friend falls in love, people often get angry and feel abandoned—especially if they're not in a relationship themselves. The stress is highlighted by the fact that they don't have what their friend has, and they fear that as their friend's life changes, they won't find a new way to connect.

These fears accurately mimic the child's. Children are so dependent that they become very vigilant, monitoring how much everyone else gets to make sure they get enough themselves. While adults don't really believe (when they stop to think about it) that there's only so much love or success to go around, it feels that way to them emotionally. They experience the situation as though they were children, vying for a finite amount of love or success.

I didn't tell Mary that she shouldn't be feeling this way. It was only natural that there would be some stress, since she had no idea what new form the friendship would take once

Jean was married. "That stress triggers jealousy," I said. I told Mary that jealousy starts in childhood, and reminded her of the rivalry that went on between her and her siblings. "You never learned to grow up to your automatic response of jealousy when you feared you're not getting enough. The trouble with jealousy is that it obscures the issue. You don't really want to take away what Jean has, do you?"

She was startled. "No, of course not."

"Maybe you couldn't control the initial reaction of being jealous because of emotional dyslexia," I said. "But you can control the aftermath. First, recognize that feelings of jealousy are a sign that you're going into a child's state. The child says, 'She has it all. If I had her life, I'd be happy. Why does she deserve to be happy when I'm not'—and so on. The more you let your mind run on in the child's state, the worse you're going to feel.

"If you look back, you can see how your jealousy progressed to anger. Anger, like jealousy, was only a signal that you were feeling deprived and were frightened of being abandoned. It seemed like a strong, empowering emotion because it revved you up. But since you had no evidence that Jean was being deliberately provocative, anger only made you feel worse. Your other option now is to assess the situation with your adult brain. Take a step away. From a slightly different perspective, you can view this as a normal change in the flow of life that doesn't reflect on your worthiness as a friend or as a woman."

It relieved Mary somewhat to know that she wasn't stuck with her feelings of jealousy and rejection. It was clear that the stress caused by her best friend's falling in love, and the subsequent change in their friendship, had driven her into a child's state. I asked her to have compassion for herself and to imagine that same compassion coming from her friend. "What would Jean say if you told her you were feeling left out?" I asked. Mary reacted with surprise. "It has never occurred to me to do that," she said. "I don't want to be thought of as a drag or a whiner. I guess she'd feel sympathetic toward me. She'd wonder what she could do to help. She'd tell me how much she cared about me." Tears came to Mary's eyes as she pictured Jean responding to her pain. She was ready to begin work.

Mary's E.D. was clearly revealed when she examined her feelings:

1. In a state of *dependency*, the child feels that happiness is contingent upon the love, approval, and constant support of another person. Mary was hurt by what she perceived to be rejection on her friend's part.
2. In a state of *distortion*, the child views herself as the center of all action, the focus of all attention. But although Mary felt as though something negative was being done to her, clearly Jean didn't fall in love in order to hurt her friend.
3. In a state of *fear*, the child feels threatened by any change in the status quo, as it is perceived as a forewarning of loss. Over time, Mary and Jean had established an intimate and comfortable way of being together, and now it was changing. Mary's anxieties were heightened by her fear that there would be no room for their old closeness in the new environment.

Using the E.D. Index, I worked with Mary to give her replacement responses to the anxieties she was experiencing. As we worked, she began to understand the emotionally dyslexic reaction that was responsible for her dramatic feelings, and to formulate the adult response that would allow her to recover her good relationship with Jean. Here is an example of how Mary used the E.D. Index:

Dependency

"Jean has found someone who loves her, but I'm still alone. Nobody wants to be with me."

Interdependency

"Seeing Jean in this relationship strengthens my belief that it's possible to form satisfying relationships. I can still feel my loneliness and longing to be in a relationship, but I can feel it with dignity."

Distortion

"Jean has withdrawn from me. She has replaced me with Ron."

Awareness

"I can be lonely and miss the good times Jean and I used to have without feeling personally slighted. Even though I miss spending as much time with her, I'm glad Jean found the relationship she's been looking for, and I know she would feel the same way if I fell in love."

Fear

"Jean makes me so jealous. She has what I want, and I'm sure that makes her feel superior to me. We'll never be close again."

Confidence

"I wish I wasn't alone, but so does Jean. Making her the enemy won't make me less lonely. Besides, just because Jean is getting married doesn't mean my life is suddenly no good."

As we worked with the E.D. Index, I could immediately see a difference in Mary's attitude. She didn't want to be stuck in a child's state of reflexive reaction. She liked the way it made her feel when she articulated adult responses. She told me, "When I look at things from the adult perspective, I feel better and stronger. This is really good. I hated being stuck with those depressed, petty attitudes. I hated feeling so jealous. I didn't want to be consumed with negative thoughts. I love Jean."

The eventual result of our work together was that Mary and Jean stayed friends, and Mary also began to enjoy Jean and Ron as a couple. She found that she liked Jean's new husband, and seeing them so happy together made her more optimistic about finding a good partner for herself.

Friendships are necessary for a good quality of life. But you need to have grown-up expectations. If your relationship needs haven't been transformed from the desire for symbiosis, you may be requiring the wrong things from your friends. Ironically, if you actually received them, it wouldn't feel too good. Adults tend to feel uncomfortable when friends are too dependent. Instead of feeling warmth, you'd feel imprisoned by closeness. Sometimes that experience can be elicited by a friend making a request you can't meet.

My client Marsha described to me how taking a trip to Europe with a childhood friend was a huge disappointment. "When Julie and I were kids, we always dreamed about someday traveling through Europe together," Marsha told me. "I can't tell you how thrilling it was to have it finally become a reality. We planned the details for two years, saved our money, and took off for three weeks last June. It was a disaster from the start." She went on to describe a series of mismatches: her friend was up early, she liked to sleep late, they couldn't agree on their sightseeing agenda, and on and on.

"I always thought Julie and I were so close we were like sisters. Since our trip, I wonder if we ever had anything in common at all."

Marsha and Julie didn't realize that being close friends doesn't necessarily mean having exactly the same needs and interests. They were afraid they'd lose their closeness if they faced their differences. Since they didn't expect differences, they weren't prepared for them, and the trip was a disappointment.

In both cases, when a friendship proved disappointing in some way, the people involved instantly called into question the entire history and validity of the relationship. I have seen lifelong friendships end over an isolated incident, the justification being: "This proves he doesn't really care about me," or, "A real friend would never say such a thing," or, "Where were you when I needed you?"

A friend's inability to help us or to meet our needs triggers E.D. Like children, we are giving adults powers they don't really have. For example, if you call a friend because you're feeling bad, only to have that friend say, "I'll have to call you back later. My dinner is burning," you can view the incident in one of two ways. You can think, "She doesn't care about me. I needed her and she wasn't there." Or you can think, "Her dinner is burning. We'll talk after dinner."

In a situation like this—and we've all had them—it's understandable to feel some discomfort. You wanted closeness and your friend was not available to give it to you. It helps to keep it in perspective: She'll call back later and you'll survive waiting. You don't have to sit and simmer. You have options: Call someone else, listen to music, or go for a walk. The problem comes when you get trapped into thinking there's only one way you can get what you need, and only one person who can give it to you. The solution is to involve your cognitive brain so you'll have a helpful replacement emotion.

The confusion we have about friendships comes from our child's brain. In childhood, our first model of closeness comes from our mother. Sometimes we play it out with friends. But we seldom learn how to "grow" those relationships. Because a friend can make us feel so good, when we're lonely we tend to give the person too much power. Then, when the friend says, "I can't talk now. I'll call you back later," it triggers a child's reaction. Once you're in the child state, it leads to a series of knee-jerk reactions, to the extent that the friend's inability to talk right now becomes:

"She could have talked if she'd wanted to."
"She doesn't care."
"Can't she see I need her."
"She's never there for me."
"What did I do to make her reject me."
"That'll teach me to depend on someone else."

And on and on, into a continuing spiral of angst—all inappropriate to the circumstances. You can see in this example how being in the child's state only adds to the feelings of isolation and separation and makes you feel worse. The closeness you originally sought when you made the call grows more and more distant.

On the other hand, authentic adult emotions allow you to feel disappointed, sad, or lonely without taking away your power. They don't debilitate you or make you a victim.

THE MYTH OF REDEMPTIVE LOVE

Be it romance or friendship, we are seduced by the notion that love has the power to make our lives complete. Many of the current self-help gurus present a message that is simple and appealing:

Love is healing.
Love is redemptive.

It's a very positive image, and one that makes sense in the context of our deep belief that love is the fundamental fulfillment of our human ego need. It's no wonder we expect love to be vindicating. All of our myths, fairy tales, and Hollywood movies—from the story of Sleeping Beauty to the movie, *Pretty Woman*—present it that way. Consider *Pretty Woman*. In the story, a prostitute meets a wealthy but emotionally guarded man. Both are shown to be deeply dysfunctional. In the end, their love rescues her from prostitution and cynicism, and enables him to drop his emotional guard and love again. This is a movie made by emotional dyslexics. It's meant to be inspirational, but ultimately, it feeds on people's despair because it says that love (and its accompanying redemption) happens by magic. But if you really examine the message, you can hear the child's voice speaking:

"If you love me enough, it will validate me and I can be worthy."
"If you love me enough, I can find personal power through your love."

But if love is so healing and redemptive, why do people find their romances and friendships so tumultuous? How realistic is the idea that love will redeem you? One of the reasons that people have so much trouble in relationships is that they expect their problems to magically disappear. Because romantic love is temporarily so divine, people think the initial euphoria will last forever. In the long run, they feel worse because the magic went away. They blame themselves or the other person.

There's no question that when you are loved, it does feel good and clean and affirming. But the difference between "child" love and "adult" love is vast and quite clear. The child's response to love is based on dependency and the need for total safety and approval. Adult love comes from the desire for appreciation, balance, and interdependency.

There's so much confusion about what constitutes a good relationship—be it romance or friendship. Our society reinforces this confusion by giving us false models for adult relationships. We buy into it and think people are behaving like adults when they're really behaving like children—examples being an overly seductive woman or a controlling man.

Think about it. It is a child's view that love equals approval. Does approval really make you feel better when you have it? Maybe initially. But ultimately, needing approval only makes you more dependent. If the person you love expresses approval, you might feel good. But what happens when he or she expresses disapproval—which is bound to happen in any relationship? Do you then question your self-worth? Do you live in fear of that person's disapproval? Do you accept her disapproval as readily as you accept her approval? You see the problem.

My goal is to help people learn to replace the child's hungry need for approval with the adult need, which is to be accepted and acknowledged for who you are. The definition of a good relationship is not healing or vindication, but a way of being with someone else that allows you to be the best "you" possible.

LESSON ONE
_____

Adult Skill: Discover Your Adultness

Adult skills don't come automatically with age. In some of the
earlier examples, you have started to get a sense of what it
feels and sounds like when you are in an adult state. But how
do you get there? The goal of the lessons in this book is to
teach you a practical formula for learning to engage your cognitive brain before you respond—to think like an adult before
you behave like a child.

The formula is simple:

1. *Stop.* Don't respond when you're feeling stressed.
2. *Review.* Observe the true circumstances.
3. *Reshape.* Determine how to make an adult response.

In this first lesson, I'll demonstrate how you can use the
formula to begin discovering your adultness. Further lessons
will show how the formula can be applied to learning a variety
of adult skills.

There are three steps to the first lesson:

1. *Stop* when you feel strong emotions.
2. *Review* the objective circumstances.
3. *Reshape* your response.

STEP 1: Stop when you feel strong emotions.

It's not always possible to be perfectly adult in every moment.
The stresses and strains of life can trigger the child's responses
in the best of us. You can't change the trigger. But even when

you're feeling highly stressed, you can learn to recognize the triggers that send you into a child's reaction, and you can choose to wait before you respond.

Remember Elaine in the earlier example? Even if she had not been able to respond reasonably to Mark breaking their date, she could have heard the warning in her strong emotions and taken a break from the conversation—perhaps telling Mark she had to call him back later. Once you recognize the signs of stress that you know are most likely to trigger a precognitive response, you can avoid a headlong collision. You can say this mantra to yourself:

> I'm feeling stressed.
> This is really upsetting me.
> Now is not the time to respond.
> Now is not the time to decide.
> Now is not the time to make ultimatums.
> I may need more information or support before I do anything.
> I can wait.

Since very few incidents are matters of life and death, chances are you can wait to give a response. It may feel awkward at first, but the results will ultimately be more satisfying than if you react in a wildly emotional way that you will regret later.

This is an example of emotional learning that you can practice every day in the most common situations. The E.D. Index can be your guide to learning when stress is interfering with your cognition. Here are some examples:

> Stress Trigger: Your husband is irritable.
> Internal Reaction:
> *Impatience:* "I need him to be loving right now."
> *Egocentricity:* "Why is he doing this to me?"
> *Melodrama:* "I can't bear this."

Stop. Do not respond, because these reactions reflect the child's impatience, egocentricity, and melodrama. You want to respond from the adult position of empathy, patience, and peace.

Leave the room or wait until you feel calmer before you respond. Once you've stopped, it opens the way to get out of the intensity of the moment and know the reality. Later, you may see that he snapped at you because he was feeling tired. Seeing him as a good person who gets tired will keep you out of the child. You can replace your knee-jerk child's responses with adult responses:

> *Patience:* "He's normally very loving. His snapping at me doesn't cancel out his usual behavior."
>
> *Empathy:* "He snapped at me because he was tired. I know he's not a mean person."
>
> *Peace:* "I don't have to let his bad mood spoil my day. It's normal for people to sometimes feel tired and upset. I can accept that."

Stress Trigger: A friend breaks a date.
Internal Reaction:
Shame: "I guess I'm not an interesting enough person."
Fantasy: "Maybe if I were different, she'd want to spend time with me."
Jealousy: "She'd rather be with someone else."

Stop. Wait until you feel calmer before you respond. Engage your cognitive brain to respond from the adult perspective of worthiness, realism, and fulfillment.

> *Worthiness:* "She did not break the date because I'm an undesirable person. Even if she doesn't want to be with me, that doesn't make me bad."

Reality: "There are lots of reasons why people break
   dates. My being different wouldn't change that."
Fulfillment: "If she chooses to be with someone else, that
   doesn't rob me of my dignity."

STEP 2: Review the objective circumstances.

It's hard to think straight when you're feeling under stress.
But you can practice by becoming an observer of others—by
watching their responses and evaluating what you see, using
the E.D. Index.

Try this experiment. For one week, make note of the
number of times you see someone overreacting to another
person's actions. Write down the incidents so they'll stay fresh
in your mind.

For example, as you go through the week observing others, you might see:

- A colleague at work blow up at his secretary because
  she didn't get a report typed in time for a meeting.
- A mother yelling at her child in the supermarket.
- An angry couple arguing on the street.
- A friend slamming the phone down on her mother.

And so on. Once you start observing, you may be surprised by how much upset there is in the everyday course of
people's lives.

At the end of the week, set aside some time to consider
the incidents you observed. Ask yourself these questions:

1. Which reaction from the E.D. Index best describes
   their behavior?
2. What do you think each of these people was feeling
   when they overreacted?

3. In any of these situations did you see people getting what they wanted?

For example:

- Did the colleague get his report typed sooner by yelling at his secretary? Or did he only create more stress that made it harder for her to concentrate?
- Did the mother in the supermarket soothe her crying child by yelling at him? Or did he only cry louder?
- Did the couple on the street resolve their differences? Or did they just go their separate ways, feeling angrier than ever?
- Did the friend resolve anything by hanging up on her mother? Or did she just make it harder for her mother to respond to her point of view?

4. What did you learn from your observations?

For example:

- "Yelling at his secretary wasn't a very good way to get something done. It only distracted her."
- "The more upset the mother became, the louder her child cried."
- "She wanted a hug, but instead she attacked him."
- "This woman and her mother weren't listening to each other. They were just banging heads."

What you learn by observing others is how ineffective the child's reactions are in solving problems. Inevitably, people do not get what they want when they react like children.

STEP 3: **Reshape our response.**

Now consider your own life, and call to mind the incidents that usually trigger emotional outbursts. Instead of beating yourself over the head for your failure to always respond effectively, begin by examining where your intent is positive. Think of a recurring stress in one of your relationships that tends to send you over the edge. Then turn the observational lens on yourself and ask, "What is my positive intent in this situation?"

Here's an example: Beverly was home with her two children all day, and by the time her husband Walter came home from work, she couldn't wait to get him involved. The minute he walked in the door, she'd start telling him about a problem with one of the children, and ask him to respond. Walter would get annoyed because he just wanted to relax. Usually, they ended up arguing, and Beverly accused Walter of not taking an active role in their children's lives. Beverly's road to E.D. was that she didn't see her husband as having needs (egocentricity). Only she was stressed and tired; he was omnipotent.

When I asked Beverly to examine her positive intent, she replied, "I want Walter to be more of a partner in caring for our children."

Once she had identified her positive intent, Beverly could move beyond frustration and blame, using her smart emotions to decide how to achieve her intent. She realized that Walter was usually a loving and supportive father, but he felt stressed when he first arrived home from work. She eventually decided that the most effective plan was to give Walter a grace period when he first came home from work, and to set aside a time later in the evening to talk about their children. Walter responded more attentively after he had relaxed. Beverly achieved her positive intent by waiting.

It's always important for you to establish the positive intent behind your reactions—and to be able to see the positive intent in the reactions of other people. If you think you're just flying off the handle because you're incompetent, or because someone else is bad, you've left no opening to resolve the problem. Identifying the positive intent gives you a pathway to the cognitive brain where a solution is possible.

> This may be a new idea for you: There is always a positive intent behind everything you do. If there's a stress in one of your relationships that you can't get a handle on, take some time when you're calm to identify that positive intent. It will give you a clue about how to solve the problem.

CHAPTER 4

Can You Be Intimate and Still Be Free?

- **Do you want to be with someone, but get scared when it happens?**
- **Do you worry that settling down means "settling"?**
- **Do you think you have to give up an important part of yourself to have a good relationship?**

Angela said of herself, "I guess I'm one of those women who loves too much." She sat in my office, a woman of thirty-seven, with an intense manner and large, sad eyes. I asked her what she meant, and she was amazed that I had never heard the term—was not familiar with the piles of literature on the subject. Of course, I did know about it. But I was curious to hear what Angela meant by that phrase "loves too much." What was her experience? Why did she think this was her problem?

She explained it this way: "Every time I get interested in a man, I let it take over my life. When I'm not with a man, my life feels balanced and sane. I go out with friends. I have fun. I work hard. But when there's a man in the picture, everything changes. I don't even recognize myself. That's what I mean by loving too much. It's impossible for me to be in love and still keep my balance."

Angela went on to describe her most recent "fiasco." She met Robert, a policeman, at a community benefit, and she liked him instantly. "You know that click you get with people, when you're on the same wavelength, and it feels like you're soul mates?" she asked dreamily. "That was the way it was with Robert and me. We were drawn to each other, and we became an item. When we were together, it was heavenly. He was a big, burly man, but he was the most sensitive lover I'd ever had. When he was at work, I thought about him constantly, and worried about his safety. He filled my life." She bit her lip, growing tearful. "But I didn't fill his. He still had his nights out with the guys, which I tried to be very adult about, but I wanted him to be with me. Then, just like that, he broke up with me. He said I was too clinging. He said I suffocated him." She nodded her head soberly. "That's my problem in a nutshell, Helen. I suffocate the men I'm with because I love them too much."

I knew one thing: Loving too much wasn't Angela's problem. There was nothing pathological or "sick" about her behavior. Very simply, she was experiencing the struggle that many people have—how to experience intimacy and still retain one's own selfhood and dignity. And chances are, Robert was experiencing similar difficulties, making it even less likely an adult relationship could thrive. It is a battle between the child who cries out for symbiosis, and the adult who needs independence. For people like Angela, it seems as if there is no middle ground. Either you get swallowed whole, or you withdraw into isolation.

Fear of intimacy and fear of being alone coexist in unhappy turmoil, and they represent different manifestations of the child's need to be cared for and his fear of being abandoned. Fear of intimacy is really fear of rejection.

For many people, the prospect of intimacy triggers enormous stress. That, in turn, triggers the child's emotional memory of a longing to be loved that went unfulfilled.

THE DEPENDENT CHILD

One of the reasons that adult intimacy poses such a problem for people is that the only model they have for being that close comes from their childhood. Children form close relationships based on total dependency. They have no way to separate intimacy from their legitimate need to be cared for. Throughout their formative years, their definition of closeness is shaped by those on whom they depend the most. Without conscious emotional learning, it is very hard for people to know what adult intimacy should feel like and how the same level of intimacy that existed when they were dependent can be maintained when they grow up.

But dependency can be a painful state even for a child. Being dependent by definition makes one vulnerable, and even the most loving parents can't be there to protect their children at every moment. When the emotional link between the parent and child is broken, even temporarily, the child is fearful. Remember, he is essentially trapped, without any options to move away, fully assert himself, or seek other caretakers.

Ideally, if the world were a perfect place, children would get their needs met so well that they would never learn that having needs and showing them was bad in any way. As they grew up, the natural process of maturation would lead to more autonomy, but they wouldn't think they had to make a choice between intimacy and freedom.

However, many children grow into adulthood without knowing how to balance their need for intimacy with the reality that life is full of separations. They conclude that intimacy makes them weak, because the only experience they have of intimacy is one in which they were dependent. People tend to adopt a polarized view of life: You can either be dependent (and thus feel constant neediness and fear of loss) or you can be independent (and thus reject intimacy as being dangerous or demeaning).

Dependency and rugged independence seem like opposite states, but they are really two sides of the same coin. When a person rejects intimacy it is because he or she fears that the outcome will be abandonment or loss of identity. It isn't "adult" to be a loner any more than it is "adult" to be overly dependent. Countless times, I have heard men and women say, "I don't want to get too involved with this person because I'm afraid I'll get hurt." They know, even as they are saying it, that this is not an empowered adult position. But they can't help it. They are trapped by past experiences of pain that they can't bear to have repeated.

In America, we live in a culture of independence because that's how this nation was born. The glories of the pioneer spirit pervade stories of our nation's settling. People came here from the "old country" with something to prove. They broke away from the traditional ways and became independent thinkers—pioneers and cowboys.

Our society has learned to value rugged individualism, something that is rarely considered positive in other countries where community and group action have been given a higher cultural value. To this day, most Americans hold the firm conviction that being able to do something alone is a sign of prowess. We see this attitude reflected not only in personal relationships but also in business, where individual ingenuity is rewarded, even if it is at the expense of others. Role models such as Donald Trump or Michael Milken reinforce the idea that you have to be tough, egocentric, and somewhat ruthless to succeed. Our heroes in business, politics, science, and just about every other cultural arena are strong, independent individuals. The man or woman who focuses on collaboration or compromise is often seen as being indecisive and weak.

In personal relationships, we live in an age of unprecedented marital failure and the collapse of the family structure where our deepest experience of intimacy took place. With some 50 percent of all marriages ending in divorce (even as more people than ever are getting married), our expectations about marriage and closeness have been challenged. Many people have concluded that the only way to maintain strength and dignity is to go it alone.

So, we're left with two messages that make it difficult to feel comfortable with our need for intimacy. One is a culture that says in order to be strong you must have no needs or dependencies. The other is the evidence we see in our families and communities that we can't count on other people to be there for us.

This is the adult dilemma: We have an organic, deep knowing that we need love and nourishment in our lives. But we can't be babies again. We can't return to the womb. Many people spend their entire lives seeking a replacement for the nurturing mother—the person who will accept and nurture them no matter what. But the truth is, adults don't really want to be treated like babies. When you think someone is smothering you or controlling you, it robs you of your power. People think you have to be either dependent or independent; there are no other choices. But, of course, there are. The true nature of the intimacy that adults seek is a transformation of the dependency they fear coupled with the freedom they so admire. Adults choose to live in an integrated state of inter-dependency, whole and real.

ESCAPE FROM INTIMACY

A few years ago, a man named Alex came to see me because he was having a terrible crisis in his relationship with Linda. Alex seemed like a nice man—open, friendly, and willing to talk. And he was obviously crazy about Linda. "We're planning to get married in the spring," he said. "Everything has been going great." He paused, embarrassed to say what was on his mind, but he finally blurted out. "This is hard. I have this problem I can't shake. One night, we were sitting in my apartment watching TV together, and I started staring at Linda's legs. I couldn't take my eyes off them. Obviously, it wasn't the first time I'd seen them, but it seemed like it. And what I noticed was that she has no . . . uh . . . curve. Bluntly put, her legs are fat." He stared at his hands, embarrassed to look me in the eye. "After that night, I couldn't stop looking at Linda's legs. It became an obsession. This is a woman I love, but my mind was going, 'How can I marry a woman with fat legs?' "

He finally looked at me with desperation. "How do I get this thought out of my mind? It's creepy, I hate myself, but it's stuck there like a big rock in the road."

I smiled at the image. It was an apt description of the way emotional dyslexia can feel. "You know what I think?" I asked Alex. "I think that Linda's legs aren't even a real concern for you."

"They're not?" He was puzzled. "So, why do I have these crazy thoughts?"

I explained to Alex that people often have irrational feelings when they're scared. It's the adult equivalent of a child's conviction that there's a monster under his bed. Alex's "monster" was Linda's fat legs.

"Do you mean I'm looking for an excuse to pull out of the wedding, without even knowing it?" he asked.

"These feelings can seem to take on a life of their own," I said. "The monster under the bed becomes the ghost at the window, then the dragon in the closet. Your fears take over. It's not rational. You'd never say to Linda, 'I'm sorry, I can't marry you because you have fat legs.' But what you're thinking is, 'I have doubts. Maybe she's not the woman for me. What if this isn't the right decision?' "

Alex sighed helplessly. "I love Linda so much. If she disappeared, I'd be crushed. But, well, it doesn't feel as completely right as I expected. I've waited a long time to get married—I'm thirty-six—and I always assumed I'd be more certain about my choice. I'm nervous that it won't work out."

I noted that in only a few short minutes our conversation had progressed from Alex's apparent disgust with Linda's fat legs to a deeper, more genuine concern over the real issue of adult intimacy. I was glad he'd come to me, because I could see his problem was one of emotional learning and could be helped. He had been reluctant to say out loud that he was bothered by Linda's fat legs. Even in the privacy of my office, he recoiled from an admission that he thought made him appear to be a bad person. Indeed, had he revealed his concern elsewhere, it might have quickly been labeled bad. I could well imagine a different reaction that began with the words, "What's wrong with you?" Or "What a jerk!"

I asked Alex to step back and observe himself, using the E.D. Index. "See if you can write your internal dialogue from the child's state, then we'll work on a more appropriate adult response," I suggested.

He was willing to try it, and was surprised to learn the depth of his worries about taking such a serious step as marriage. Here's what he found:

1. In the child's state of *dependency*, Alex felt that marriage meant losing himself—that Linda would want all of him, and he would want all of her.
2. In the child's state of *distortion*, Alex believed that adults were supposed to know exactly what they were doing, that "true love" was always supposed to feel right, that there would be no accompanying ambiguity or discomfort.
3. In the child's state of *fear*, Alex felt that his needs could be dangerous; if they didn't get met, it was because they were not good.

As we worked together, Alex began to see that his irrational focus on an imperfection in Linda was an unconscious effort to make her less desirable so that he wouldn't be hurt when she found him in some way undesirable.

Instead of telling Alex he was wrong to have such a seemingly shallow obsession, I tried to elicit the underlying feeling that the obsession represented. Once Alex was persuaded to talk about his deeper fears, Linda's legs became a nonissue. An encounter with intimacy can be scary, especially for someone who thinks marriage means the merging of two individuals into one whole. Alex was able to see that adult intimacy could be nonthreatening. It could strengthen the self, not destroy it.

This is the replacement dialogue he wrote:

> "As an *interdependent* adult, I can relate to Linda as my partner, and ask for her support. I don't have to be perfect, and I don't need her to be perfect, either."
> "As an *aware* adult, I can keep things in perspective. I know that life has its ups and downs, and Linda and I don't have to have a fairy tale marriage for us to be good together."
> "As a *confident* adult, I know that Linda loves me for myself, and I needn't fear that she'll leave me."

Alex's replacement dialogue was a beginning. In the future, whenever he felt the old childlike emotions coming to the surface, he could stop and engage his cognition to put himself back on track.

THE SEX-INTIMACY CONFUSION

Although the words *sex* and *intimacy* are often used interchangeably, most people know that intimacy is much more than sex. Nevertheless, it is often in the sexual arena that men and women are most starkly confronted with their unresolved childhood needs and the feeling that they may engulf them.

An adult with emotional dyslexia enters a sexual relationship with a basic sense of dependency, which makes him or her feel unworthy. This manifests itself in many ways—from pursuing sexual conquests randomly to withdrawing from sex altogether. Having sex without intimacy is the way some people retreat from revealing themselves. The paradox is that in trying to protect themselves in this way, they ultimately get labeled as unsatisfactory lovers by their partners. As such, they receive the rejection they're trying to avoid in the first place.

Some people use sexual desirability as a way to escape feeling unworthy. For a child, touching is essential, so it's a very powerful trigger for E.D. Being desired is an affirmation, and it's easy to make the mistake of thinking that sexual activity can confirm one's desirability. Indeed, it can do just that—briefly. But if it is not accompanied by intimacy, which affirms one's self beyond sex, it ultimately becomes nonaffirming. For example, the woman who is desired by many men because of her great beauty eventually feels used.

At the same time, men are socialized from early on to believe that a good man is one whom women will want to sleep with. They feel tremendous pressure to perform. While a woman can feel good by being held and cuddled, often a man can't. What sometimes happens in relationships is that women feel victimized and pressured into having sex. If they go along, they're resentful of the man and angry at themselves for being so needy that they don't have enough self-control to say no. They're frustrated because they're not really getting what they need.

Geraldine was a woman in her mid-forties who had been married to Alan for fifteen years. They had two children, and she told me right up front that she felt they had a very stable marriage. But Geraldine was troubled, as she had been for most of her marriage, by the fact that Alan wouldn't talk to her about "important things."

"When I was young, I had a picture of the way my husband and I would be," she said. "We'd share our most intimate thoughts; we'd sit and talk about philosophy and the meaning of things. We'd tell each other secrets and talk openly about our love. Instead, I married a completely noncommunicative man. The only conversations we ever have are about the kids, the house, or the state of our bank account. I feel starved for meaningful conversation. From Alan's standpoint, the most terrifying words I can utter are, 'I want to talk.' He thinks I mean that I want to bitch at him about something. Most of the time, I feel invisible to him. I have no idea what he's thinking, and it hurts me that he doesn't seem to care what I'm thinking. But after an entire day of ignoring me, he considers it perfectly reasonable to go to bed and want sex. For me, sex isn't satisfying without talking and intimacy. I end up feeling used, and he can't understand why I'm so angry. He doesn't have a clue."

This is a common theme between men and women. Because women so often experience intimacy through talking, they assume that when men don't talk about their feelings, that means they're being cold and distant. But men aren't very good at intimate talking because they're not socialized to express their feelings. Women would feel better about the men in their lives if they looked at their actions, not their words.

I think of a woman named Ruth who complained that her husband refused to talk about sex. She related how she sat down and tried to have an honest heart-to-heart conversation with him about their sex life, and he just shut her out. "He didn't care about my needs," she concluded bitterly. "I told him I wanted more touching and closeness, and he mumbled something vague to placate me, and turned on the TV."

Ruth was angered by what she regarded as coldness on her husband's part. Yet, as we talked, she began to describe a trip they took to a country inn the following weekend. On the trip, her husband made love to her, and there was a lot of the touching and closeness she had asked for. He was very passionate and romantic. But she was still angry at him because he wouldn't talk to her about it.

"Ruth," I exclaimed, "listen to what you're saying. You're saying that your husband gave you exactly what you asked for, but you're angry because he wouldn't talk about it. You got the result you were looking for when you initiated the conversation, but you're still focused on the conversation. Read his behavior, not his words, or lack of them. Your husband made sure his feelings were expressed behaviorally, and you can't see it because you're stuck on wanting to hear the words. You've lost sight of the fact that you got what you wanted."

Because sex is one of the primary ways adults express and experience intimacy, it becomes a potent trigger: Am I normal? Am I desirable? Does he want me? Does she find me appealing? Is my body sexy? We are aided in our fears by a sex-crazy society that sets us up for disappointment by encouraging us to compare ourselves to arbitrary standards that are impossible to reach. The result is that at the slightest hint of sexual trouble, people jump to melodramatic conclusions: "I'm not desirable." "He doesn't want me." "I can't perform." We have taken one of the richest human opportunities for intimacy and turned it into a war game.

Michele thought she and Tony had a problem with sex after three years of marriage. But they discovered it was really a problem with their different styles. When Michele first came to see me, she was almost ready to give up. "It used to be that Tony couldn't keep his hands off me," she told me shyly. "I think he's grown bored with our sex life." She described to me how on many nights she would go to bed and lie there waiting for Tony to join her, hoping he would be in the mood for sex. "He'll be in the study working on his computer, and he'll say, 'I'll be in soon.' But I lay there getting more and more frustrated. Then I cry because I don't think he wants me anymore. Then I get angry and he doesn't understand why I'm angry. I'm usually asleep by the time he comes to bed, and when he wants to have sex, I'm not in the mood anymore. I feel like I'm just a convenience to him."

As we talked more about their lives, I learned that Michele was a very busy magazine editor, who hopped out of bed at six every morning and rushed off to work. Tony was a writer who preferred to work in the evening. Their schedules were mismatched, and Michele was aware of this, but she hadn't made the mental leap to thinking they also had mismatched schedules when it came to sex. The subject of sex was so volatile, so wrapped up in issues of identity and worthiness, that she had completely separated it from the picture. In other words, their difficulty finding time to have dinner together was viewed as a scheduling problem, but finding time to have sex was an emotionally charged issue. Once I established that their marriage was solid in other arenas, I suggested this to Michele: "Maybe you need to schedule a time to have sex."

She was surprised to hear this. Like many people, she believed the romantic, but entirely impractical, notion that sex was supposed to always happen spontaneously. I asked Michele to examine what was really happening on those nights when she was in bed feeling frustrated and Tony was at his computer.

"Here's one possibility," I said. "You're lying in bed, waiting for Tony to join you. The longer you lie there, the more upset you get. You think Tony is deliberately snubbing you, that he's sitting in his study thinking, 'I don't want to have sex with Michele, so I'm going to stay out here.' But everything else you've told me about your marriage suggests that isn't true. In fact, Tony may feel the same way when you jump out of bed and rush off to work in the morning."

"But I'm not snubbing him then," she protested. "He knows I have to get to work early."

"And you know Tony works best at night, so why don't you assume the same thing about him?" I asked. "Here's another explanation you can consider: Tony is not sitting in his study trying to avoid having sex with you. He may not be thinking about you at all. Maybe he's involved in his work, and his failure to come to bed has nothing to do with sex."

Michele was a smart woman, but this explanation had never occurred to her. Her emotional dyslexia led her to make automatic assumptions about Tony's motivations that were totally unsupported by the other evidence. What Michele and Tony were experiencing was a common mismatch, and one that could be solved with scheduling. I asked Michele if there was a time during the day when it would be comfortable for them to have sex. She was a little bit embarrassed with the idea of planning sex, but she had to agree it made some sense. She thought about their schedules and said that there were two hours every day between five and seven in the evening when they were most relaxed. That became their time for sex. Problem solved.

As long as Michele thought Tony was doing something to her by working late at his computer, she was trapped in the child's view: If you don't meet my needs, you must be saying that my needs are bad.

This is a good example of how emotional dyslexia drives a wedge between two people. Locked in her hurt feelings, Michele was turning away from Tony in the mornings when he approached her sexually. Her explanation—"I have to work"—sounded like rejection to him, just as his explanation—that he worked best at night—sounded that way to her. Because they were both thinking like children ("If my needs aren't met, my needs are bad"), there was no chance they would solve their problem.

The situation was further exacerbated by the distinctly male-female way they handled the problem. Michele would lie in bed crying at night, then grow angry and defensive in the morning. Tony simply withdrew deeper into his private world. Because men and women tend to respond differently to the same feelings—in this case, rejection—they can only reach common ground by tuning themselves in to the other's way. If Michele had known that Tony's withdrawal was in response to his hurt feelings, instead of assuming he didn't find her attractive, she would have had an easier time helping him and herself.

The most common sexual problem that couples have is that they're having very little or no sex at all. Old inhibitions and feelings of badness left over from childhood interfere with intimacy. The fact is, you have to be an adult to have satisfying sex. You're not going to get it if you're living in the child state.

A vivid example of this came to me through Donna and Frederick, a young married couple who consulted me. They had both grown up in troubled households, and had gone through a great deal of therapy, both individually and as a couple, to come to terms with painful past memories. In particular, they said they had been helped by John Bradshaw's "inner child" therapy, which put them in touch with their childhood selves.

But Donna and Frederick were having a problem they couldn't resolve. Inexplicably, they had stopped having sex. "We don't understand what is happening to us," Donna said shakily. "We have never felt so close, so intimate. We have discovered deeply meaningful things about our pasts. We have cried together about our childhoods and helped one another relive the pain. But when we try to have sex, we can't. What's wrong with us?"

Donna and Frederick may have found a new level of intimacy as they came to terms with their childhood hurts, but it had become the sole basis for their relationship. As gently as possible, I told them, "You have made your deepest connection one of relating as children. And children don't have sex."

Donna and Frederick needed to learn new adult ways of being intimate. Sex wasn't the problem. The issue was to find ways of caring and sharing as adults. Once they did so, they spontaneously began to feel sexy again.

"TELL ME EVERYTHING"

In the passionate closeness that marks the early stages of love, couples actually feel as though they are two parts of the same whole. You hear expressions like, "We're like peas in a pod," or, "We're joined at the hip." In the beginning, a couple might tell each other, and really mean it, that they will always share their deepest thoughts and sentiments, in a spirit of openness and honesty. But these magical times eventually give way to reality, and the idea that sharing equals intimacy becomes explosive.

When people tell me they think it's very important to share some potentially explosive revelation with a partner, I always ask, "What's your motive for telling? Why do you want the other person to know this?" I see that they are confused by the difference between confession and sharing. Making a confession is different from sharing information about yourself that will enhance your relationship. Sharing is a generous act that arises from a feeling of goodness. A confession often comes from the sense of shame and is made in the hope that the other person can redeem you by saying you're okay. Children make confessions because they depend upon approval. Adults share to communicate.

Not long ago, I watched a television report about a new form of couples therapy whose premise was that intimacy equals honesty. This therapeutic approach called for couples to always tell each other exactly what they were thinking at the moment the thought occurred, or soon after—no matter how hostile, angry, or rejecting the thought might be. Several couples appeared on the program to say how employing the technique of brutal honesty had saved their marriages.

In one particularly memorable segment, a man revealed to his wife that when he was making love to her the night before, he had been fantasizing about an old girlfriend. His wife accepted this information with a smile. Her reaction: He was being honest; therefore, his comment was acceptable. It didn't feel very much like real life to me. Although most people know that such fantasies are normal, they don't necessarily like to be told about them.

Those who practiced this approach thought of themselves as real adults because they could handle their partners' honesty with abiding equanimity. But, in fact, they were actually re-creating the child's state. They were looking for approval—the kind a mother gives her baby that is total and unconditional. Asking for that approval is a sign of emotional dyslexia, because a lover isn't a parent, and you're not an infant. Your lover isn't going to unconditionally approve of every word you utter.

As adults, we know that our words and actions make an impact on others—something a child isn't aware of. The "total honesty" movement is a denial of that fact. It's the old child's cry of, "If I feel it and think it, it must be valid"—and it's okay to express it whenever it pops up. Inevitably, people who tell all don't receive the affirmation they desire. Interdependent adults, who can share their thoughts and feelings in the spirit of goodness, are responsible for the effect they have on others. They don't need the constant reassurances of total honesty to make them feel loved.

ACHIEVING INTIMACY IN INTERDEPENDENCY

Most of us have a pretty good idea of how people behave when they are in the child's state of dependency, or in the companion state of rugged independence. But what exactly is interdependency? How does it appear in a relationship, and how do you achieve it?

The E.D. Index offers some clues. Let's elaborate on the comparison between the child's state of dependency and the adult state of interdependency. (Remember, dependency sometimes manifests itself as independence.)

Dependency

When you're dependent, you are actually afraid of getting too close. You're constantly on your guard to protect yourself from what you think is the inevitable rejection. This fear makes you cling to the object of your dependency, who is the source of your approval and good feelings.

You end up feeling diminished by your feelings of dependency, or obsessed with keeping your distance to prevent being swallowed up.

Interdependency

With interdependency, you enjoy the rhythm of closeness and autonomy. You can experience intimacy as satisfying, as well as doing things alone. You find that it's nice to be by yourself—reading, walking through a museum, sitting in a park—and it's also nice to share time with another person.

You can be a partner to another person—spouse, colleague, friend—and be satisfied by the way you can help and be helped by one another. An interdependent person actually feels enhanced by others' strengths.

The good news is that it is possible to have an intimate partnership and still maintain your dignity as an individual. In fact, that is the only way adults can have satisfying relationships. When you come to a relationship as an authentic adult, with a sense of your own and the other person's worthiness, the relationship can nourish you to be the best person you can be. In the following lesson, you'll learn skills for loving that will make intimacy enriching rather than fearful.

Adult Skill: Achieve Intimacy Without Losing Your Power

As Alex, the man obsessed about his financée's legs, found out, it can be utterly confusing to fall in love. In my experience, it's one of the most stressful events in a person's life. The initial euphoria sends a flood of signals to the brain. Fear vies with ecstasy. Confusion reigns.

Intimacy is stressful. It's a powerful trigger for the child's reactions. That is why it's so important to learn how to engage your adult cognitive brain when you're in an intimate situation. This lesson will teach you how to do that. There are three steps, using the formula of stop, review, and reshape.

1. *Stop* and prepare to be in love.
2. *Review* what constitutes adult love.
3. *Reshape* love as an adult.

STEP 1: Stop and prepare to be in love.

You won't find adult love when you're looking for it as a child. If you're not currently in a relationship, but want to be, you can begin by clearing your brain of all the child's negative messages. If you blame your own unworthiness or the unworthiness of others for your lack of success in forming relationships, you've already set yourself up for failure the next time around.

What are the negative messages? Here are some examples of statements I hear all the time, along with replacements that express the adult counterparts.

STATEMENT: "I haven't had a date with a man for almost a year, and I'm so lonely."

The child is saying:

"I'll never find anyone!"

The adult responds:

"I wish it was easier for me to meet men. I may need to get some help."

STATEMENT: "Another man I care about has left me."

The child is saying:

"There's something wrong with me. I'm too needy, and men can tell."

The adult responds:

"Maybe I'm choosing men who aren't available, or who are unnerved by my intensity. I act intense because I'm lonely. Maybe I need more time with friends so I'm not so intense."

STATEMENT: "My best friend just got married. I'll never find a man unless I lose at least twenty pounds."

The child is saying:

"I have to be perfect to win a man's love."

The adult responds:

"I wish I was planning my wedding, but a crash diet isn't the solution. Besides, I have friends who are in good relationships, and they're not perfect. Being twenty pounds thinner might make me feel better, but it won't make me more lovable."

STATEMENT: "Another woman turned me down. Women aren't attracted to me because I'm not rich and successful."

The child is saying:	*The adult responds:*
"If I were more successful, I'd be comfortable with women, and I think they would find me much more appealing."	"Maybe I don't come on like gangbusters, but I love my work and I know plenty of women who find that quality appealing."

STATEMENT: "My girlfriend is always criticizing me. I just can't figure out what women want."

The child is saying:	*The adult responds:*
"Relationships are too confusing and dangerous. If I can't figure everything out, I won't have control."	"She has good intentions, just as I do. We both want love and companionship, but we sometimes have different ways of expressing our needs."

Take some time to think about where you might be letting negative attitudes interfere with your readiness for relationships. Remember, you can't be in an adult relationship if you do not come to it as an adult. Keep in mind your positive intent. It's good to want an intimate relationship. Your negativity stems from wanting that good thing so much that you let it trigger childlike reactions.

After you've written down your negative attitudes, use the E.D. Index to formulate replacement responses. The positive you is the authentic adult you. That's the person who can enter a satisfying relationship.

STEP 2: Review what constitutes adult love.

The emotional triggers that accompany love are so strong that most people think feeling dizzy, confused, and anxious are natural to the love state. Unfortunately, they also find that these emotions get in the way of having satisfying relationships. The precognitive childlike emotions that signaled love when they were children haven't been transformed into the smart emotions that allow them to make good choices. What happens with many people is that they lose the rational ability to determine whether or not they're experiencing authentic love—whether the relationship they're in will be enduring and enriching or emotionally exhausting and short-lived.

Since our culture is so loaded with fantasy images of "true love," it's not surprising that it would be hard for people to recognize when love is real. But right from the start, during the time when you think you're falling in love, you can use your cognition to replace the child's feelings of *dependency*, *distortion*, and *fear* with the authentic adult's feelings of *interdependency*, *awareness*, and *confidence*.

In fact, there are many clues that are easily discernible if you step away from the emotional flurry and use your cognitive brain to evaluate a relationship. If you are in love now and aren't sure if this man or woman is right for you—or if you are hoping to enter a relationship in the future—take some time to distance yourself and reflect on the following issues. They will serve as a guide to whether your love is experienced from the child's viewpoint, or from the state of authentic adulthood.

Child Love	Adult Love
DEPENDENCY: governed by shame, victimization, and impotence	INTERDEPENDENCY: governed by worthiness, freedom, and power
You feel insecure if you don't spend most of your time with your partner, enjoy the same activities, like the same people, and so on. You are frightened by differences. They seem threatening.	You operate in a healthy state of interdependency, which leaves space for you to be fully realized individuals. You understand that this makes you more loving partners. Differences are not threatening.

You give up important parts of yourself to have a relationship. You can't believe that someone would want to be with you the way you are.

DISTORTION: governed by egocentricity, impatience, and fantasy

You maintain your dignity, and bring your best self to a relationship because that's the only way it is fulfilling.

AWARENESS: governed by empathy, patience, and reality

You're worried that you won't have another chance for intimacy. You think you're getting too old or are not desirable enough. You are disheartened by your past failures.

You can feel good about yourself whether you're in an intimate relationship right now or not. You know that you'll be able to find a relationship in the future because relationships don't occur by magic.

You base your connection on superficial qualities that seem appealing in the beginning, but may fade with time. Ask yourself: Can you be with this person if he or she is sick, has financial problems, grows older and becomes less beautiful, etc.

FEAR: governed by rigidity, jealousy, and melodrama

You often feel that you're in a state of melodrama about your relationship—fighting, withholding sex, crying. In the beginning, the drama might feel good because it seems to match the positive passion you feel. But eventually, it leaves you feeling upset much of the time. You never feel entirely secure, and aren't sure how to recognize whether things are okay or not.

You understand that a lasting love requires acceptance of the complexities of adult living. You are willing to embrace the inevitable adult issues together.

CONFIDENCE: governed by flexibility, fulfillment, and peace

You have conflicts, because that's a normal part of life. But you keep them in perspective, and even use them to learn more about each other. You have a sense of humor about the ironies and quirks of living. You know that life can sometimes be funny, and that human beings are never entirely predictable.

Authentic adult love enables you to be more generous, open, engaged in the world around you. Childlike love isolates you and makes you unhappy. You don't have to be helpless when you fall in love. As an adult, you can use your cognitive skills to evaluate whether it is right for you. Most of the people who attend my singles groups complain that they can't find a partner, but the real issue is being ready to be in an adult relationship and learning to recognize when that relationship is based on adult sensibilities. Finding and keeping a good relationship becomes a natural outcome of adultness, rather than a desperate, hungry pursuit.

Step 3: Reshape love as an adult.

Once you've completed the work of being an observer of the child and the adult responses to love, and practiced making the distinctions in your own life, you're ready to make an adult choice.

If your relationship history has been marked by failure interspersed with long dry spells, you might wonder if the good relationship you seek will always elude you. In my work with single men and women, I have found that, once they learned adult skills, they were able to find good relationships. Here's an example of the way one woman used smart emotions to overcome her child's way of being in relationships—and finally found a good partner.

When Miranda first joined my singles group, she said she liked men who were "free spirited, a little rebellious, and unconventional—usually artists or musicians." At the time, Miranda was thirty-five years old and had just ended another in a long string of relationships—this one with the leader of a blues band.

Miranda was a real head-turner, a beautiful red-headed woman with huge expressive eyes and a vivid personality.

She always took center stage when she spoke in the group. We listened to her stories of doomed love, and she made people laugh with the ironic twist she gave to her tales. It was like listening to the Perils of Pauline. But the bottom line was, Miranda was there because she wanted an intimate relationship and she couldn't seem to find one that endured. She conceded that she had a pattern of choosing men who fled from commitment, but beyond that, she was stumped. "What can I do?" she asked breathlessly. "You can't help who you fall in love with."

One week Miranda came to the workshop, fresh from a trip to the West Coast, and started talking about a man she'd met on the airplane coming home. "We really enjoyed each other's company," she said. "I have to say I liked him. He was very funny and smart. He asked me for my phone number, and I gave it to him, but I don't know . . ."

"What don't you know?" I prodded.

"Well, he's a stockbroker, for godsake. Can you imagine me with a stockbroker? And he's not my physical type at all. He's short and kind of paunchy."

I decided to take a chance and try something with Miranda. "I have an assignment for you," I said. "You say he's not your type. Just this once, go out with someone against your type. Pretend you don't have any preconceived notions about what your type is, and just see how you feel when you're with him. You might even want to write some things down after you go on a date: Did you like the way you were with him? Were you interested in what he had to say? Did he listen to you? Since romance is so emotional, it can help to turn on your rational brain. Do you want to try it?"

Miranda shrugged. "Why not? Okay, I'll try it. It'll be different."

Six months later, Miranda announced that she was marrying her stockbroker.

What happened? Once Miranda set aside her rigid notions of the kind of man she thought she needed, she found a man whom she could love. She made a transition from childlike fantasy and rigidity to adult flexibility and reality. Many people have never stopped to consider what actually feels good to them in a relationship. They've always looked outward for clues, depending on looks, status, and other superficial qualities to guide them. They have no idea how to evaluate their inner feelings.

You can engage your cognitive brain to find out how to make a choice that feels good to you. Using Miranda's experience as a model, perform an experiment: Go on a date with a man or woman, whether or not they are your "type." After the date, take some time to evaluate what the experience was like:

1. Describe the way you felt with this person, using the E.D. Index. For example, would you place your emotions in one of the child states or in one of the adult states?
2. Did you like the way you were with this person? Did you feel like a confident adult or were you a nervous wreck?
3. Make a list of the positive and negative aspects of the experience. Place each point on the Child or Adult side. For example:

CHILD	ADULT
It made me uncomfortable to be taller than he.	He listened to what I was saying, and seemed to appreciate my sense of humor.

4. What have you learned from this experience about making adult relationship choices?

Adult love always occurs when you are in a state of *interdependency* (not feeling too weak), *awareness* (not being unrealistic), and *confidence* (not feeling fearful or threatened). As you begin to recognize the differences between making decisions based on childish thinking and adult thinking, your intimate relationships will make you feel more—not less—powerful.

CHAPTER 5

Can You Be Alone and Have Dignity?

- **Does love seem to be something magical and elusive?**
- **Do you know more about why your personal relationships have failed than how to make them succeed?**
- **Does everyone but you seem to have someone to love?**

When I conduct singles workshops, the majority of the men and women who attend say they're sad about being alone. They can't figure out why other people can find partners, but they can't.

Often, they have explanations that blame men for being too distant or shallow, or women for being too pushy or picky. Blame helps them cover up their own feelings of shame ("Something is wrong with me because nobody loves me") by making it someone else's fault.

I sense a deep anxiety in the room during these workshops. It's not always a palpable presence, but I can see the pain in the way some of the participants express themselves: The woman who talks about always choosing inaccessible men. The man who admits he withdraws every time a relationship starts to get serious. The woman who thinks she can't find a man because she isn't pretty enough. ("That's all men care about," she says.) Or the man who is certain he would have women following him down the street if he had a full head of hair and was six-foot-two.

The fundamental fear is: "I have a terrible flaw that makes me unlovable. I'll always be alone." And yet, here they are, these groups of single men and women, working hard at finding what they want, and committed to being in relationships. Why else would they be there?

I look around the room and see a group of men and women who are no different from any other group one would see at the theater, in a restaurant, or in a class. They have no obvious flaws that would single them out for a lonely life. Despite the fear that pervades their descriptions that they are "on the blink" when it comes to the opposite sex, there's nothing about them that supports this premise. In fact, in any other context, many of them would be considered winners.

A majority of the people who attend my singles workshops are professionals who feel quite confident when you ask questions about their work. Joel is a classic example. I found his words particularly poignant as he talked about his success—and his loneliness. "Everyone thinks I've got it made," Joel said. "I don't get invited places because they assume I must have other plans. It's true, at work I'm a dynamo. But what people don't realize is that I go home at night, open a beer, and sit in front of the television all alone."

When I asked Joel why he didn't try to initiate something, or even let his friends know he was feeling lonely, he answered with remarkable honesty, "People count on me to be strong. If I show weakness—God forbid, if I admitted I was lonely!—they'd think less of me. I'm no dummy. I know this line of thinking is getting me nowhere, but I can't seem to get past it. It feels safer to let things stay the way they are."

Feelings of loneliness don't just happen to "losers." They can happen to anyone. In fact, all adults feel lonely sometimes. It is a common trigger for the child's reactions. In Joel's case, his fear of looking weak had been responsible for a number of failed relationships in the past. He tended to choose women who were dependent because it made him feel strong, but ultimately their dependency weakened him because he could never give them enough and could never get appropriate support from them. Joel's fear also carried over into his job. Although he was a powerful man who had achieved much in his career, he unconsciously avoided hiring strong people to work for him, and this undermined his business. Now he was feeling lost and lonely because he had avoided having people around him to whom he could relate as equals.

But there was another reason for Joel's relationship problems—something I encounter often in singles groups. Although they don't always admit it up front, most of these people tend to have fairly rigid ideas about the type of person who would make a good partner. Based on past experiences, they've defined the "type" of person to whom they're attracted. This definition can be as general as "someone in the arts," or as specific as "he has to be six feet tall." It's not that they're narrow-minded. They honestly believe that they're only capable of falling in love with or being sexually attracted to a certain type of person.

Speculation about that elusive quality known as romantic chemistry has baffled scientists and poets alike. In my experience, "chemistry" is based on a similarity according to where you fall on the emotional dyslexia continuum. As we discovered in Lesson Two, people who don't have adult skills haven't transformed their childlike needs into adult needs, and they're more likely to rely on superficial qualities in a partner. Basically, they don't know what would satisfy them if their needs were "grown up." So they look for mates through a child's notion of romance. They don't know themselves well enough to pick partners with whom they'll share something deep and lasting.

People are aided in their childlike perceptions by a myriad of cultural prejudices that limit them. We are bombarded by society's ideals of men and women—especially the way they should look. Rationally, we might understand that the way a person looks is an insufficient indicator of how that person might be as a partner. But we are swept up in the cultural standards. I have had men tell me how good they feel walking into a room with a beautiful woman. It's like a sign to others that they're good enough to attract her. Women talk about having the same feeling when they're with a handsome man. People feel validated by the way their partner looks to others, which is a way of covering their own shame that they can't measure up themselves.

Furthermore, the idea that only a certain type of person can attract you and be suitable for a relationship is a child's way of expressing rigidity and of narrowing options. In a convoluted way, it feels safe to pick a type and stick with it. But it doesn't necessarily lead to satisfaction, especially if the "type" you've chosen is consistently unsuitable.

I was reminded recently of how easy it is for people to feel bad about themselves based on arbitrary standards. A friend of mine returned from vacation and we were talking about her experience. My friend is a voluptuous woman who has been fighting a weight problem all of her life. Like most women, she had learned to think of being thin as the objective standard of female beauty. But she noticed something on her vacation that allowed her to see it in a different way. "When I was in Upper Volta, the men paid so much attention to me," she said. "They thought I was beautiful. The whole time I was there, I felt like the ideal woman, because in Upper Volta people with my body type are considered more sexually desirable and womanly. But then I went to the Riviera and, just like that, I was invisible. Men didn't look at me. There, being attractive meant being thin."

Society gives us guidelines for being humiliated. It's so easy to feel bad about yourself when the ideals are arbitrary and impossible to meet. But beneath all the blame and frustration is the core feeling that if you don't have a romantic partner, you're not good enough to have one.

In particular, women are conflicted about being alone. The combined forces of socialization and biology bear down on them with the message that they must fulfill a preordained destiny, which includes being a partner and mother. Now, they're being given new messages that promise them greater fulfillment if they break away from the old patterns. But often, they end up feeling confused and betrayed because they don't know how to integrate their roles. They're not happier. They're alone. They don't feel more fulfilled.

The people who come to my singles workshops don't want to hear platitudes. They feel that it rings false to repeat the mantra that they're okay, that they don't need a mate to feel good about themselves, that they're attractive and desirable just as they are—and so on. While it may be true on a fundamental level, these images don't square with the pervasive cultural messages they're bombarded with every day—the messages that still say a woman isn't complete without a man, or that a person who is alone is unsuitable. That's why the psychological work they've done in therapy falls short. It doesn't close the gap between what they feel and what is evident all around them. There's a missing link in the adult educational process that leaves them still responding with helplessness and fear, and they tell me they can't "snap out of it."

One of the problems with most popular psychology and self-help theories is that they tell people that self-esteem comes from within; you gain self-esteem first, and then you're able to relate to others. This just reinforces the isolation people already feel. I don't believe that self-esteem can be achieved when you're sitting alone in a room because it isn't something you can magically "will." Self-esteem is a by-product of relating to other people as an adult.

LONELINESS TRIGGERS THE CHILD STATE

There are few experiences that are as uncomfortable as feeling lonely. That's why it's such a powerful trigger for childlike emotions. Remember, the child cannot bear loneliness. He needs constant support from the outside to reassure him that everything will be okay. For example, when a child feels sad, he has no inner resources to help him get out of that state. He can't use his cognition to help explain the circumstances, or tell him that his sadness won't last forever. He feels lost in his feelings. Children are vessels too small to hold the pain of giant, scary emotions. They don't have enough "self" to put things in perspective. They are unable to see things in the context of the future, because the future doesn't seem like a real thing to them.

The adult, on the other hand, has memory and perspective. He knows that sad feelings don't last and that crises pass because he has experienced them before. An adult may be heartbroken over the loss of a love, the death of a parent, or any other real-life trauma. But experience has shown that the intensity of the sorrow will eventually lessen and may eventually disappear. It takes time.

When people are not taught how to feel their loneliness without the panicked sense that they'll never get out of it, it triggers E.D. Either they deny the validity of their feelings, or they cling to relationships as though their lives depend on them—whether those relationships are healthy or not.

A couple of years ago, I started giving a workshop for people who were involved in obsessive relationships because I noticed it was such a common theme. These were relationships that were unfulfilling, destructive, and debilitating, yet still people were hanging onto them for dear life. When they ended, the people involved could not emotionally let go of them, even though they usually admitted the relationships had not been good for some time. I saw that there was a connection between an apparent fear of being lonely and the tendency to become involved in (and stay involved in) hurtful relationships. The memory of being unloved in the past was so painful that these people would do anything to escape having that feeling repeated.

Maggie was a case in point. She came to the first workshop, a woman of forty, who exuded sensuality and intelligence. There was also a sense of drama that surrounded her, as though she were engaged in the fight of her life. "I'm a normal woman," she told the group. "But I was involved with a man for more than a year who wouldn't have sex with me."

She told this story: "Bill and I met at a business conference a year ago last summer. There was an immediate spark. Bill's ideas about marketing were creative and exciting to me. I'd been surrounded by so many dull minds. And we hit it off personally, too. It seemed natural to start seeing each other outside of work, and before long, we were in bed together." Her eyes gleamed with the memory. "Sex with Bill was terrific, and I know it sounds corny to say it, but I think what made it so good was the fact that we could relate on so many other levels. It was the most complete relationship I had ever had. I knew I was falling in love, and I thought Bill was, too. We were so perfect together. It never occurred to me that he might not feel the same way. Two months after our affair began, he said he didn't want to have sex with me anymore."

Maggie was fighting back tears at this point, and the people in the group leaned toward her with interest and compassion.

"Of course, I was stunned," she went on. "I wanted to know why . . . what I could do to fix things. Bill just told me point blank that he wasn't in love with me, and he thought it would be better if we just stayed friends.

"I didn't believe him." She looked around the group and added defensively, "It wasn't because I was deluded. It's just that Bill's other behaviors didn't square with what he was saying. Except for not having sex with me, nothing else changed. He didn't walk away. He didn't go out with other women. He seemed to want to be with me. We worked together and played together. Our friends treated us like a couple—I'm sure they all assumed we had a sexual relationship. We took vacations together. Over Christmas, we went skiing, and last spring we went to Mexico. On those trips, we slept in the same bed. We hugged and cuddled and acted intimate in every way except sexually."

I interjected at this point. "So, Bill said he wasn't in love with you, but you thought he didn't mean it?"

Maggie shrugged helplessly. "What else was I going to think? I figured he was one of those men who got scared when things heated up, and if I gave him time, he'd come around."

"Did you talk about it?" I asked.

She nodded wistfully. "Every so often, I'd bring it up, just to see if he was ready. I tried not to be too pushy. Sometimes I couldn't help myself. I just blurted out, 'I love you.' Bill would get real cool and say, 'I've been clear with you about how I feel. I don't know what I can do to help you with this.' Every time this happened, I was crushed all over again. What was going on? What was he doing to me?

"The thing is, when I really thought about it and was honest with myself, I knew what I should do. I should walk away. I wasn't prepared to live forever with a man who wouldn't have sex with me, or who obviously wouldn't make a commitment. But every time I imagined myself actually leaving, I felt completely panicked."

Maggie took a deep breath and wiped her eyes. "Well, it probably won't surprise you to hear that he left me a year ago. He simply announced that he'd fallen in love with another woman and he was going to get married. I know it's hopeless—I'll never have him—but I can't stop thinking about him. Even though he's married now, I dream about him showing up on my doorstep, saying he's made a terrible mistake and really wants me. I feel so sad and alone that I don't see how I can ever recover." She blushed. "Sometimes I call his machine, just to hear his voice, or walk down his block, hoping to catch a glimpse of him. I'm completely out of control, and I know it."

Maggie's story was a textbook case of obsessive love. The fear of being without the object of that love was so overwhelming that she continued to immerse herself in thoughts and dreams of him long after there was any chance they would be together.

One woman in the group said, "Why do you love him? He dumped you. You're a terrific person. You shouldn't let him take that away from you."

Others nodded in agreement. Although they had similar tales to tell, they could objectify the experience through Maggie. It seemed clear, when it was happening to someone else, that it was futile to pursue a love obsession that brought nothing but pain. The women in the group were eager to boost Maggie's confidence by convincing her that she didn't need Bill to make her happy. But it wasn't that simple. In some way, being with Bill had made Maggie feel fulfilled and happy. Even after he stopped having sex with her and told her he wasn't in love with her, she found so much that was positive about the relationship that she clung to the idea that everything would work out. Her terror now was that the only person on earth who could make her feel that good was Bill, and he was gone.

I began addressing Maggie's crisis by focusing on the positive. "Tell us what it was about Bill that was so special," I said. "What was different about this relationship from every other one you've had?"

Her face grew animated. "I felt so alive with Bill," she said. "There was so much passion. All of my previous relationships—including a five-year marriage—didn't have that.

I'd never experienced it before. And I was so sexually turned on by Bill. I guess I hoped and expected that we would start having sex again. We were so intimate in every other way, it only made sense."

"I understand," I nodded. "It's certainly reasonable that you would want to be with a man who made you feel alive and passionate."

She looked at me with surprise. "It's funny that you would say that," she said. "All of my friends think I'm nuts or self-destructive."

"It's not self-destructive to want the feeling of fulfillment you had with Bill in the beginning of your relationship," I told her. "The problem is, you think you can only have these feelings with Bill. We're going to make sure you keep that sense of vitality and fulfillment in your life—even without Bill."

I was glad that Maggie had come to my group. One function of the group was to help people see that what they thought was their own personal pathology was really an issue for many other people. All the people who were there had had relationships like Maggie's. Each one had experienced the feeling that a particular man was like a magnet pulling her. Even though things got worse and worse, she couldn't stop it, and ended up feeling like a lunatic.

It was revealing that when I asked these people how soon in their relationships they knew it wasn't going to work out, they almost always replied, "Right away," or "Soon."

What made them override their own intuition and stay with people they knew would eventually break the connection? What often happened was that they felt controlled by their feelings of desire because they liked themselves so much when they were in an intimate relationship. They liked the feeling of closeness, but most of all they enjoyed the way they were during those times—generous and full of warmth. But they assumed, as Maggie did, that they were dependent on the other person for those feelings, and this triggered childlike feelings of fear and neediness.

I told Maggie and the others in the group, "You can approve of yourself for wanting to be intimate, because it's a wonderful side of you. You know, part of intimacy is the experience of generosity—'because I feel good, it's a pleasure to be good to you'—and that's also a wonderful quality. Who doesn't want to have such rich human emotions?"

I turned my attention to Maggie. "When you were with Bill, you experienced all the positive outcomes of being intimate. But you were also in a panic because if Bill left, you believed he'd take them with him. When he did leave, you felt hopeless because you thought you had lost your chance for passion and aliveness. It was as though the intimacy was a precious jewel that he gave to you, then abruptly took away."

To show Maggie and the other people in the group that they could have intimacy without having the man with whom they were obsessed, I asked them to concentrate on other relationships in their lives. Romantic relationships were so full of emotion for them that they couldn't be intimate without also feeling dependent. For them to see that they could have the experience of intimacy without the craziness, they needed to practice on less-threatening relationships. I asked them to think of other people in their lives with whom they were intimate—a friend, sister, niece—and to describe how it felt to be with that person. As they spoke about these loving relationships, I heard them describing the full warmth and richness of love, and their expressions were devoid of any panic.

"That's what you can have with a man, because that's who you are—generous, giving people," I told them. "You just need to learn how not to have your dependency button pushed when you're in a romantic relationship."

Maggie experienced this herself a short time after the workshop when she took a trip with two old friends from college. By then, she had a general predisposition to see herself as a good person, not a failure. As a result, she felt her warmth toward her friends and theirs toward her in new ways—how much they had shared since they were in college together, how much they liked each other. Maggie still wanted a man in her life, but she was beginning to learn that her obsession had stimulated negative feelings, not the positive feelings she felt with her friends. Now she could begin to look for a relationship with a man without feeing so needy. Falling in love didn't have to send her reeling.

STAY IN A STATE OF WORTHINESS

When you're feeling lonely, it can be hard to think well of yourself. A friend once described a particularly low period in her life when she felt isolated from everyone around her. She was working very hard during the week, but it seemed on the weekends, everyone had their own plans. "Last weekend, the phone didn't ring once," she said, as evidence of her isolation.

I happened to know that this woman was an exceedingly warm and generous person, who had many friends. But she'd recently ended a long-term relationship, and she was experiencing the discomfort and sense of instability that periods of transition often bring.

Loneliness can bring up the child's melodramatic responses to the point where you live in a constant state of injury and neglect. It's easy to slip into the feeling that nobody really cares, that your friends have deserted you, that nobody loves or understands you. Life seems dramatic, and ordinary things take on extraordinary significance. For example, if you feel lonely, the sight of a loving couple walking down the street can generate fierce pangs of isolation.

Emotional dyslexia sets in motion a series of automatic reactions to the behavior of others. When you feel as though you have been injured, ignored, or insulted, see if you can find other explanations for the behaviors of your family and friends. Don't immediately assume that because you feel hurt, it was their intention to hurt you. The difference between a child and an adult is that you have the resources to look beyond black-and-white explanations.

Maybe you can relate to these examples:

- Your friend promises to call, but doesn't.
- A friend forgets your birthday.
- No one thinks to invite you to their home for the holidays.

Any one of these situations can trigger childlike responses. The temptation to feel hurt is perfectly understandable, because we all want to be surrounded by expressions of love. But before you conclude that the actions of others are deliberately designed to snub or injure you, ask yourself:

- Is this friend normally loving and considerate?
- Was it this person's intention to hurt you?
- What are other possible explanations?
- Does this incident affect your basic goodness?

Since emotional dyslexia causes us to react instinctively and see ourselves as being threatened by the behaviors of others, most people haven't learned to consider other explanations. If you have a friend who is otherwise thoughtful and loving, and she doesn't invite you to her party, or she forgets to acknowledge your birthday, it's highly unlikely that she has suddenly decided to hurt you, or has stopped caring. Once you acknowledge that, you are free to stop feeling hurt.

Self-affirmation doesn't happen in isolation. Most people find it hard to maintain a feeling of self-worth without the sustenance of others. Humans are oriented toward community, and that is where we thrive. It's our nature to be social beings. But sometimes, people let feelings of loneliness over-whelm them to the point where they don't seek out the very environment that would nourish them. Don't let loneliness become a trigger for being isolated. Rather, let it serve as a sign that you are a normal human adult who needs the sup-port of others.

Adult Skill: Remember Your Worth When You're Feeling Low

It's a fact that every human being feels lonely sometimes. It doesn't matter if you have many close friends, or if you're on good terms with your family, or if you have a loving partner. But when you have adult skills, you learn that the emotions that often accompany loneliness (such as jealousy and shame) are signals that you're moving into the child's state, and shouldn't be trusted as real. You can halt the plunge into hopelessness before it takes hold. As an adult, you have the power to do something about your loneliness. You can replace it with the rich adult feelings of warmth, generosity, and love that are part of the real you.

The biggest challenge for people is how to hold onto their feelings of worth—that is, to express adult emotions—when the objective evidence of their lives seems to be telling them otherwise. This lesson will teach you how to replace your reflexive reaction of self-denigration with a more empowering response to troubling situations. There are three steps to this lesson:

1. *Stop* when you hear your E.D. triggers.
2. *Review* the positive dimension.
3. *Reshape* a dignified response.

Step 1: Stop when you hear your E.D. triggers.

First, I want you to begin listening for the flag words or phrases that signal when you have E.D. It's a good idea to write them down. These can be things others say or they can be internal responses that you have. You'll find that the more you learn to recognize the words and phrases that stimulate the child's reactions in you, the less potent will be their effect. By doing this work, you'll know when you're heading into the child's state, and you'll be able to find adult replacement responses.

Examples of your negative triggers might be:

"I'm too fat."
"I can't compete."
"I'm a failure."
"I always screw up."
"It's all my fault."
"Nobody loves me."
"I'm a fraud."
"If people only knew the real me . . ."
"I'm too weak."

You can add others. This is the internal dialogue that drives the message of inadequacy deeper into your psyche. The more you reiterate these messages, the weaker you become. They are the precognitive child's way of perceiving discomfort. Inadvertently, you reinforce them by dressing them up in adult language to make them feel more real. But if you can recognize them as E.D., you can use your cognitive brain to maintain your adult dignity.

1. Find each of your E.D. signals in the E.D. Index. For example:
   Egocentricity: "It's all my fault."
   Impotence: "I always screw up."
   Shame: "If people only knew the real me . . ."
2. Write down what the adult replacement response would be. For example:

"It's all my fault."
(Egocentricity)

"I feel bad right now because
I'm missing something I need.
That doesn't mean I *am* bad."
(Empathy)

"I always screw up."
(Impotence)

"Everyone makes mistakes,
but I have choices about how
to fix this. I can get some help
from others." (Power)

"If people only knew the real
me . . ." (Shame)

"I am a worthy person who
deserves to be loved."
(Worthiness)

STEP 2: Review the positive dimension.

As I have said before, it is impossible to hold onto the empowering adult emotions if you are trying to do it alone. But since there isn't always a friend available to be supportive, this step in the lesson enables you to hear your supportive friend's voice whenever you feel a negative trigger.

Once you have listed your E.D. responses, try to remember a situation in which you experienced feeling that way. For instance, you might recall feeling rejected when a man didn't call you, or ashamed when you overheard someone commenting on the weight you gained. Remember the internal dialogue? Maybe you thought, "I'm unlovable," or, "I'm disgusting."

Now, I want you to alter the image. Pretend that a dear friend is describing the very same situation to you. Choose someone whom you care about, and whom you see as a very good and worthy person. As you imagine her describing her feelings of humiliation, ask yourself how you would respond.

Most likely, you would say something like, "Of course, you feel disappointed. He promised he'd call and he didn't." Or, "Of course, you were uncomfortable when you heard someone say you were fat."

I call this the "of course" response. You would naturally

feel great empathy and understanding for a friend who is trying to confront such a problem, because you know your friend is good and worthy, and this situation doesn't change your attitudes and beliefs about her. It certainly doesn't make her a terrible person. You feel compassion for her.

Let's help you to experience the same compassion. If you wouldn't judge a dear friend as unlovable or disgusting, why would you judge yourself that way?

One way to help yourself hear the compassionate voice is to choose a person, real or imagined, whom you feel to be strong, loving, and supportive. It could be a teacher you once had, a close friend, a therapist, your grandmother, or even someone from a book or movie. Pretend you are describing a disappointment to this person, and listen to him or her give you the compassionate "of course" response. For example:

"Of course, you feel lonely since Fred left."
"Of course, being sick makes you feel weak."
"Of course, it's painful when you overhear someone say-
    ing you're fat."

Hearing the "of course" response begins to restore your sense of dignity. It helps you acknowledge that difficult situations are naturally going to give rise to uncomfortable feelings—but those feelings are not there because you're worthless. They're simply the automatic reaction anyone would have. "Of course" validates your feelings, and it also leaves an opening for you to respond differently.

When you are having a hard time remembering how much you are loved, you can also engage your cognitive brain to stimulate positive memory. Flip through your address book, noting the names of the people who are listed. Remember things they have said to you that were affirming, such as: "I love to talk to you when I'm blue, because you always say something soothing." Or, "You're so much fun." Or, "Spending an evening with you is such an invigorating experience."

Precognitive emotions make you forget. Engaging your cognition helps you remember.

STEP 3: Reshape a dignified response.

If you're like most people, you aren't used to thinking about loneliness as dignified. You focus on what's missing from your life and think, "Because I need a good relationship and I don't have one, there must be something wrong with me."

Remember, the child views her unmet needs as being bad and making her bad. She thinks if her needs were good, the all-powerful adults would meet them. An adult with E.D. feels the same way.

To hold onto your dignity, you must listen to your needs from the adult state. In this step, I want you to make a "needs collage." Find pictures or words that describe the things you really need in life, such as a satisfying job, an intimate relationship, good friends, children, a chance to use your talents, and so on.

Each of these needs reflects a positive aspect of the good person you are. Once you have built your collage, consider how each need is good. For example, imagine a friend saying to you:

"Being satisfied with one's work is a basic human motivation."
"Every adult needs intimacy. Your need for intimacy is an expression of your adultness."

Keep the collage in a prominent place to remind yourself that your needs are not signs of weakness, but rather they are empowering aspects of yourself. When you recognize and affirm your needs, you can begin to make choices that will enable your needs to be met.

> If you describe life's difficulties as being the result of your fundamental badness, there is no open doorway to change. Only when you are given positive, affirming responses to your adult needs can you live happily in the adult world, seeking and accepting all of the options that are available to you.

CHAPTER 6

Can You Accept Differences in Others?

- Do you feel that the closeness in your relationships is easily disrupted by disagreements?
- Do you only feel comfortable when there is perfect agreement?
- Do you think people have to be alike to be happy together?

People often have the mistaken idea that closeness comes from sameness. They think that when two people are together, they're automatically supposed to enjoy the same things, have the same reactions to family events, like the same friends, share the same political ideals, and so forth. This idea is based on the subconscious assumption, "If you're the same as me, I must be good; if you're different, I must be bad (or you are)." Ordinary conflicts between people with different styles become the source of serious problems in relationships. Emotional dyslexia drives people to make negative judgments when they're unable to accept the differences.

That was the problem with Rachel and her husband Bob. When Rachel came to see me, she declared, "Bob is about to drive me straight out of my mind. Bob and I love each other, and we're happy most of the time. But we have these petty arguments, and they're upsetting. Bob's a real perfectionist. I'm not exactly a slob, but living with Bob can be like being in military boot camp. Everything has to be in order every minute. My attitude is, if it doesn't get done today, it will get done tomorrow. I won't leave a wet towel crumpled on the floor, but I won't necessarily hang it so it's at exactly the right angle, either.

"Look," she added, "I don't want to make too much of this. The truth is, I wouldn't even care about Bob being a neatness freak if it didn't cause me so much angst. I have plenty of stress at my job, but he's constantly on my case, and it's exhausting. For instance, the other night while I was eating a bowl of ice cream, I suddenly remembered that I'd promised to call my friend Lynn. I put the bowl in the sink and went to make my phone call. When I came back, the bowl and spoon were washed and Bob was fuming. I wasn't in the mood for a fight, but he goaded me into one by lecturing me about my sloppy habits and why couldn't I take a minute to wash the bowl . . . blah, blah, blah. I blew up. I said, 'Don't you think calling a friend is more important than washing a dish?' He said, 'What's the big deal? It would have taken you five seconds.' He just didn't get my point at all, and I sure as hell didn't get his. It ended with me calling him a fanatic and storming out of the room. The evening was ruined. Even the next day, when I tried to discuss how miserable he was making me with his compulsory neatness, he wouldn't budge. His attitude was, there's a right way to do things and a wrong way to do things. No negotiation. No amnesty. His way or the highway. He said, 'If you cared enough, you'd do it.' One side of me can't believe we're fighting over stuff like when to wash a dish. But the other side of me feels hurt. Bob's disapproval can bring out my insecurities faster than anything."

I was intrigued by Rachel's account of her domestic crisis because it was such a clear example of how hard it is for people—especially those who have chosen one another as mates—to accept the differences between them. Both were trying to erase their sense of badness by being right. Rachel's story shows how dangerous it can be when people don't have adult skills—how much suffering it can create. People see themselves as having loving cores, but then their differences trigger crazy, angry responses, and the loving cores seem to disappear. Rachel was less upset about Bob making an issue of the dirty dish than she was about what she projected for the future. I'd seen it a thousand times. I knew she was thinking, "If he's this way about the small stuff, what will he be like when we have a real crisis?" Bob may have been thinking the same thing about Rachel.

But viewed objectively, Rachel and Bob are simply people with two different styles, and neither style is better or worse than the other. Order and cleanliness are very important to Bob; in these areas he is a perfectionist. Those same details mean much less to Rachel; calling a friend is a greater priority than washing a dish. Overall, they have a good, strong relationship, but their different styles create a lot of unnecessary tensions.

I told Rachel, "You think it's stupid to feel angry and rejected because Bob criticizes you about leaving dishes in the sink, and you also think Bob is stupid for making an issue of it. But let's examine this. Have you thought about why you react this way?"

She considered my question for a moment. "I guess it's because I love it so much when we're feeling close. It's so good being with Bob, and most of the time he makes me very happy. I love Bob, and I know he loves me. But when he yells at me about leaving a dish in the sink or not making the bed the correct way, I see red. He makes it sound like a big deal. I start wondering if we're really right for each other. If he can't accept me the way I am, how can we live together?"

"Have you ever wondered why it's important for Bob to have everything so neat?" I asked.

She shrugged. "It's just the way he is, I guess."

"Think about it, Rachel," I said. "It wouldn't be so important to him if it didn't provide a positive benefit. I think the first thing you have to do is find out why he feels so strongly about this. Perfectionists are expressing their nature. The behavior means something to Bob. He's not deliberately trying to hurt you. He's only trying to get some need met. If you find out more about how he feels, you'll be able to get on track. See if you can get him to tell you how it feels to him when the house is a mess."

Two weeks later, when we met again, Rachel described her conversation with Bob. "I asked him straight out, 'How do you feel when you come home from work and the house is messy?' He looked at me like I was nuts. And he was awfully suspicious. This has become such a sore subject for us, I think he thought I was setting him up for another brouhaha. I convinced him I was serious, and he actually started to talk about it. He told me things I hadn't known before."

"What did he say?" I asked.

"He said that having a neat environment helped him feel calm. He described it as a physical sense of well-being. For him, mess stood for chaos. He had a lot of stress at work, and he liked the way it felt to come home to an orderly environment. He said he was surprised I couldn't figure this out, because his mother is a well-known pack rat. Their house was always piled high with stuff she brought home from flea markets and yard sales.

"As Bob and I talked about how uncomfortable he felt growing up, I really understood for the first time why he's so neat all the time. He's obviously afraid things will get out of control and he'll end up living in a mess again." Rachel smiled at me with relief. "It was a good conversation, Helen. I think he also got the point that when I leave a dish in the sink to talk on the phone, I'm not driving a stake through his heart." She laughed. "In other words, I'm not deliberately doing it to cause him pain. I told him that I got the same feeling of calm when I returned phone calls—like straightening up my relationship environment."

Rachel and Bob discovered that they both had a need for calm. They just achieved it differently. But where could they go with this realization? Clearly, knowing you have conflicting needs isn't enough to solve a problem. But I find that when normally caring people discover how their actions have a negative impact on others, they try to adjust their behavior because they're able to see each other's positive intent. That's what happened with Rachel and Bob.

Once Rachel and Bob were able to appreciate that they had different styles, without judging each other as right or wrong, they discovered new options. Rachel could decide to straighten up the house as a loving gesture—comparable to bringing one's mate flowers—knowing that it would soothe Bob and put him in a good mood. Likewise, Bob could linger at the dinner table and talk, knowing that the dishes would get done and the mess wouldn't get out of control. These adult responses broke through their automatic E.D. reactions—which were to blame or to feel inadequate because the other person was different.

THE RIGID, JUDGMENTAL CHILD

Differences make people with emotional dyslexia feel very uncomfortable. Often that discomfort leads them to make negative judgments. The child's voice says, "If you and I are not alike, one of us has to be better and one of us has to be worse." And so they choose. Usually, the other person is worse.

A child has a limited view of the universe, with little

input from the outside. The unfamiliar is scary. For example, a child might start crying or stare in awe and fear at a nun dressed in traditional garb if he has never seen one before. He'll hide behind his mother's skirts if he sees a disabled woman in a supermarket, and steal glances from a safe vantage point. The child doesn't have the cognitive skills to know that what is unfamiliar is not necessarily threatening.

Children get a lot of reinforcement for their rigidity from emotionally dyslexic adults who fear differences themselves. If you are taught that someone is threatening because of his race or religion, or that a certain political philosophy is more righteous, you'll hear these as truths in childhood. The same beliefs get carried into adulthood if you never learn to formulate your own reasoned ideas about the world around you. Most adult societies tend to be highly suspicious of people who don't fit the prescribed norm—whether that norm is racial, religious, or physical. In a sense, people are trying to erase their sense of shame by shaming others.

If you are like most people, you make automatic judgments every day, based solely on the fact that the people you meet or see on the street are different from you. A man in a wheelchair is helpless or sick. An obese women is a slob. If you have adult skills, you might override your initial instinct and stop yourself from continuing the judgment. For example, your first reaction of pity for a man in a wheelchair might be replaced with an interest in understanding what his experience is like, or respect for his ability to maneuver under difficult circumstances. But if you have not learned to see differences as a part of life and as an opportunity for learning, such encounters only deepen your discomfort and tendency to be rigid.

A good example is the way many people respond to homosexuals. With the burgeoning of the gay rights movement and the threat of AIDS, homophobia has grown more widespread. When many people encounter a gay man or woman, they are immediately flooded with a whole series of responses and fears:

"This person is disgusting."
"How can she be that way?"
"It's wrong."
"He's dangerous."
"He doesn't belong here."
"Keep him away from my children."

And so on. These responses reflect the child's state of fear. People feel threatened by homosexuals and defend their position by saying, "Homosexual behavior is not normal." But the idea that only the "norm" (or majority behavior) is acceptable is based on the rigidity whose basis is fear.

Infallibility does not exist. Adults know that life isn't black and white, and norms are human-made constructs that are not in themselves right or wrong. Minorities are not less human or their needs less valid because there are fewer of them, and there is a wide array of differences that exist within every norm. While it may feel safer to label others based on their class, race, religion, looks, health, or other criteria, the real result is that it makes life more, not less, dangerous. It drives people apart and makes confrontation more likely.

Let's use the E.D. Index to show how an encounter with differences feels to an adult with emotional dyslexia:

Dependency:
"How can you approve of me if we are different?"

Distortion:
"If you have different needs, how am I going to be sure *my* needs will get met?"

Fear:
"If there are no rules for what's right, things will get out
of control."

The authentic adult, on the other hand, is able to put
differences in perspective. Again, using the E.D. Index, see
how the authentic adult responds:

Interdependency:
"I don't need your approval to be acceptable. I am happi-
est when you accept me the way I am."

Awareness:
"I can find ways to get my needs met, and respect your
separate needs, too."

Confidence:
"Life is filled with ambiguity. Sometimes that's uncomfortable, but it's not dangerous."

MEN AND WOMEN IN CONFLICT

The biggest conflicts that I see in my practice are between men
and women who just can't relate to the ways that separate
physiologies and conditioning contribute to differences between the sexes.

Most of the women who come to me with relationship
problems cite the age-old stereotypes of the men in their lives:
distant, afraid of commitment, critical, controlling, and so on.
They can't understand why men behave the way they do—
especially how a man who may seem so sensitive, loving, and
passionate one moment can be so cloddish, cold, and distant
the next.

My male clients have quite a different set of age-old stereotypes concerning the women in their lives. They think

they're often flighty, mercurial, whimpering, and overly demanding. Their most common plea is, "What does she want from me?"

We saw an example of typical male/female ways of responding with Rachel and Bob. When Bob was uncomfortable, he became critical and controlling. He lacked the language of feelings that would have allowed him to tell Rachel why a messy house upset him. Rachel read Bob's criticism as demeaning and hurtful. She felt attacked, and because she loved Bob so much, she saw his criticism as directed at her very being, not at the mess she had created. Theirs was a classic case of a man and woman mired in emotional dyslexia. Neither could respect the other's differences. They sought solutions through confrontation—exactly the opposite of what ultimately worked. I have seen many couples like Rachel and Bob, whose lives are a morass of hurt feelings and misunderstanding. They are like emotional ships passing in the night, neither one seeing the other's point of view, each perpetually wounded by the other's actions.

Here are simple examples of how a man and woman might respond differently to the same situation. Notice how their reactions are different variations of E.D.

Situation	Expression	Reaction of the Other
He has a good time on a date.	He pulls away so he won't seem needy or unmasculine.	She feels he really doesn't care and was only toying with her.
She has a good time on a date.	She daydreams about the future. She waits for his call or invents reasons to call him.	He feels she's too needy or pushy.

He wants to be helpful.	He tells her what to do to solve her problem.	She doesn't feel comforted. She wanted sympathy, not instructions.
She wants to be helpful.	She shows warmth and sympathy.	He feels babied and embarrassed.
He's tense.	He drives fast and curses the other drivers.	She feels he's being hostile, and maybe it's directed against her.
She's tense.	She cries.	He feels irritated and burdened.
He's stressed at work.	He comes home and puts on the TV to unwind. He doesn't want to talk.	She feels rejected.
She's stressed at work.	She comes home and wants to talk about what happened and how she feels about it.	He feels overwhelmed and unable to help.
He's concerned about their child's poor grades.	He tells the child to buckle down and work harder.	She hugs the child and offers to help with the homework.
She's concerned about their child's poor grades.	She wants to have the child evaluated and treated. She blames the incompetent teachers and lousy school system. She thinks he's being too hard on the child.	He thinks she's coddling their child and overreacting.

Men and women have both told me they think it's hopeless to try and connect with one another. But what they perceive as different needs are simply different ways of expressing the same needs—and often, different points of entry into the child's way of responding. For instance, a woman who thinks she is being ignored by her husband might burst into tears, while he may react to that very same sense of insecurity by becoming silent and withdrawn.

Over the years, I've often worked with couples whose mismatched responses to crises make the situations worse. As one woman complained, "I feel like we're from different planets!" When I helped them to see why their different responses were attempts to accomplish the same positive goals, they were able to bypass their instant childlike reactions of, "You don't care" or "You don't understand."

Holly and Barry are a case in point. When Holly learned on a visit to a new doctor that she had an ovarian growth, she was, rightfully, quite upset, especially since she had been getting regular checkups and her previous doctor hadn't diagnosed the growth earlier. When she came home and told Barry, he immediately flew into a rage against the original doctor, going on and on about how incompetent he was. Holly was appalled that Barry was not trying to comfort her. Couldn't the doctor wait? But Barry, who was conditioned to defend, was focused on the desire to protect his wife from the bad doctor.

When Holly tearfully told me Barry's reaction, she said she felt that he was more concerned with the doctor's possible malpractice than in how she was feeling. I suggested another explanation. "Maybe Barry was being helpful in the only way he knew how—by trying to protect you," I said. "It's a natural male instinct to protect a loved one. His anger at the doctor was in defense of you. It was what he could do right then and there. So he did it. You needed to give him another way to help. Sometimes you have to tell a man what you want. The next time, say, 'I'm upset now, and I just want you to hold me.' "

Another couple, Laurie and Sam, had a similar experience when they learned that their college-age son had gotten his girlfriend pregnant. Sam raged loudly and Laurie wept quietly. She told me that she didn't recognize her ordinarily mild-mannered husband. "He was so angry," she said. "He gets that way from time to time and it scares me."

"Men don't know the meaning of a good cry," I said. "Crying helped you release some of the stress you were feeling. But men rarely release stress by crying. They're more likely to become angry. If we tell men it's wrong to release their stress by getting angry, it's the same as their telling us we shouldn't cry." I suggested to Laurie that instead of being afraid of Sam's anger (which didn't escalate beyond a brief episode of yelling), she should accept his method of venting frustration.

I asked Laurie, "Would you really want Sam to react the same way you did to being upset? Would you want him to burst into tears?"

She had to laugh at the image, and admit that no, it wouldn't be his style at all. She could also acknowledge that his way of expressing frustration was healthy, not harmful.

Men and women can learn to see one another's unique approaches to pain, without judging them. They can read the underlying positive message—"He's trying to help"; "She's feeling frustrated and needs an outlet"—without being threatened by them. They also need to celebrate the way the sexes differ, because it is actually one of the great riches of a relationship.

The Prince or the Frog

It's understandable that there's some confusion when men and women get together, since they have different approaches to life. The bookshelves are lined with the psychology of re-lationships—books that try to explain the underlying (usually destructive impulses responsible for their baffling behavior. The problem is, many of these books (usually written for women) only feed their anger and frustration by describing men as immature (*The Peter Pan Syndrome*), or overly hostile (*Women Who Can't Say No and the Men Who Abuse Them*), or psychologically flawed (*How to Live with a Passive-Aggressive Man*), or weak and undeserving (*Women Who Love Too Much*).

These books try to dispel the myth that men are omnip-otent and women gain their power only in relationship to them. But in the process, they tend to set up scenarios that lack any of the ambivalence of real adult life. Women who have catered to weak, controlling, or abusive men have been termed "codependent," once again using a pathological model to explain a lack of skills. Women are encouraged to "cure" their codependency by forsaking many of the charac-teristics that make them unique. Thus, a warm, supportive woman gets labeled codependent if she behaves in a nurtur-ing way. The end result is that many women are confused. They don't know how to express love and still remain strong.

I find that when we shift the focus from pathology to emotional learning, both men and women are empowered to be more effective. Pathological explanations only cement the victimization that people feel.

Not too long ago, I worked with a woman who described herself as codependent. Fifteen years earlier, Harriet had been married to an alcoholic and she'd joined a self-help group to help her make the decision to leave him. In the group, she was told that she had been enabling his addiction—thus the label codependent. She'd also been told that she was code-pendent—in other words, "addicted" to being in relationships with the wrong kind of men.

By the time she came to see me, Harriet was a veteran of many self-help groups, all focused on her so-called codependent personality. It had become the excuse for everything she had not achieved in her life, and she viewed it as the reason for her failure in relationships. I saw immediately that by pursuing this pathological explanation, Harriet had grown afraid to be herself. She questioned her instincts constantly, and every time she felt loving, she wasn't sure whether it was real love or merely the old "pleasing" behavior of the codependent. She couldn't really get her life in order until she learned to make a distinction between expressing love and the pleasure of doing things for others, and her codependency.

When she came to me, Harriet was in a state of nervous anxiety because she had just met a new man, and she was afraid of repeating her old patterns. She wanted to show him the warm, generous side of herself, but she also wanted to express her strength. She asked me, "How will I know the difference?"

I wanted to move Harriet out of the pathological mentality that the word *codependent* suggested. It only made her feel weak and incurable. Instead, I taught her about emotional dyslexia and began to build a different framework for her thinking.

To ease her anxiety about her behavior, I gave her the simple test described in Lesson Two: "If you wonder whether your loving behavior is coming from strength or weakness, ask yourself, 'Am I doing this from confidence or from fear?' " As we talked, Harriet began to think back to her marriage, and she realized that much of her behavior had been generated by fear. "I wasn't an enabler," she said, beaming with the new awareness. "When I took care of Eddie and made excuses for him and treated him with kid gloves, I was just trying to fend off his rages. I guess I was acting from fear, but I confused it with love."

Today, men and women have overdosed on pathologically based pop psychologies that categorize all behavior into dysfunctions. The result is that the sexes feel more hostile toward one another than ever. There is little room for achieving common ground or even understanding that differences are okay and a part of life.

I'm not suggesting that every mismatch between a man and a woman is tolerable. You have to evaluate your situation and decide if the differences between you can be transcended by the overall goodness of your relationship. Sometimes, the core difference—be it in fundamental values or style—is just too great.

Most of the time, it is my experience that men and women really want their relationships to work, and they're willing to make the changes involved in doing so. But they often lack the adult skills that help them distinguish when a mismatch is too great to continue. Susan had that dilemma. After years of involvement with unfaithful men, Susan was thrilled to meet Alan, who seemed truly devoted to her. She was very excited when he asked her to move in with him a few months after they had met. This felt like "true love" to her. She tried to ignore the fact that Alan was judgmental and visibly uncomfortable with her friends, her musical gifts, and her displays of affection. Susan muffled her intensity because she didn't want to drive Alan away, but deep down, she didn't feel right about it.

When I worked with Susan, she revealed that the tendency to bury feelings was an old family tradition. In her childhood, the unspoken message had been: "I'll love you, but only if you don't rock the boat." Susan was replaying that familial bargain with Alan. In exchange for his "love," she was masking her intensity and, in effect, pretending to be someone she was not. In our work together, I focused on Susan's good intentions. I asked her what it was like with Alan in the beginning.

"He was great," she recalled. "Funny, smart, cute. He seemed to really like me, and that made me feel so special."

"How is it different now?"

"Well, he's a lot less interested in my music, which was

a big draw for him in the beginning. He thinks my style is a little abrasive. We're a lot different than I thought we were."

"Does it bother you?" I asked.

"Sometimes," she acknowledged. "But I know Alan. I remember how sweet he's capable of being. I think in time he'll relax and it'll be okay again."

Listening to Susan, I wondered if this mismatch might be too great, but I could understand why she was determined to try. Her memory of the early days when Alan seemed devoted was so strong that she kept trying to get it back. Now, instead of questioning Alan's criticism, she questioned herself. I saw that she needed to be reminded of what someone who loved her was like. I encouraged her to talk about her relationships with the close friends who enjoyed her personality and talent.

"What would your friends say if you stopped playing music or you held yourself back from giving them the big warm hugs they've come to expect from you?" I asked her.

Susan scoffed at the very idea of such a thing. "They'd assume something was wrong," she said. "They'd hate it. Those parts of my personality are what they like about me."

"Precisely," I answered. "If someone is frightened of your self-expression, that's probably too deep to change. The security you feel with your friends is a model of the security you will feel with an adult relationship. That's your point of reference. Can you see Alan responding to you like your friends do?"

Susan eventually decided on her own that she and Alan should part. Because she was learning adult skills, she was also able to avoid blaming Alan or herself. "I guess we wanted different things," she said. "It wasn't anyone's fault."

A NEW BALANCE OF POWER

When you judge others because they are different, you rob them of dignity and diminish your own power in a situation.

"Shaming" others only reinforces your fear that you too will be shamed. As an authentic adult, you enter a relationship with a sense of rightness. You don't need the other person to provide it. You don't have to constantly be on guard, fearing that the other person will stop loving you. Two people with different styles but a common point of love and respect can build an environment for each other that is quite rewarding. Their conflicts do not have to drive them into the child's state. Their life need not be a seesaw, always forcing one person up and the other down, but rather, a balanced, safe place to be.

Adult Skill: Accept Differences Without Judging

Accepting peoples' differences doesn't have to mean that you're not discriminating, in the positive sense. You can make choices and judge what works for you and what doesn't. But when you make negative judgments based on dependency, distortion, and fear, you rob other people of their dignity.

Judgmentalism always comes from the child:

1. In the child's state of *dependency*, you need validation for the way you are. When others are different, it triggers your reaction of *shame:* "I must be inadequate."
2. In the child's state of *distortion*, differences trigger a reaction of *egocentricity:* "Your behavior is always about me. Everything you do is about me."
3. In the child's state of *fear*, differences are always threatening. The child believes the only way to be safe is to react with *rigidity:* "Only my way is right."

Once you understand that negative judgments always reflect the child's view of the world, you can begin to learn how to replace them with the authentic adult responses. There are three steps to this lesson:

1. *Stop* when you hear an E.D. judgment.
2. *Review* the positive adult replacement.
3. *Reshape* a positive "match."

STEP 1: Stop when you hear an E.D. judgment.

For one week, make a note of every time you judge someone negatively. This can be an instinctive reaction to someone you pass on the street, an angry reaction to a loved one, a judgment about a political figure, or even a reaction you have to a character on television or in a movie. Engage your cognitive brain to be an observer of yourself. Write down your judgments. For example:

"She really let herself go."
"He's such a baby. Why can't he be more supportive?"
"The president promised to fix the economy and he really screwed up."
"She has it all."

At the end of the week, examine your reactions. Find each one of them on the E.D. Index. For example:

"She really let herself go."	= *Shame:* "Fat people are unworthy."
"He's such a baby. Why can't he be more supportive?"	= *Egocentricity:* "His actions are designed to hurt me."
"The president promised to fix the economy and he really screwed up."	= *Fantasy:* "Problems can be magically solved."
"She has it all."	= *Jealousy:* "There's not enough to go around. If she has it, I can't."

Now, find the adult replacement for each of your reactions on the E.D. Index. For example, if you identified one of your reactions as "jealousy," the adult replacement would be "fulfillment." Restate the judgment using the adult response. For example:

Shame	*Worthiness*
"She really let herself go."	"She's struggling with her weight right now, but that doesn't make her less lovable."

Egocentricity

"He's such a baby. Why does he sulk instead of saying what he feels?"

Empathy

"He's frustrated that things aren't going well for him, but his anger is not about me."

Fantasy

"The president promised to fix the economy, and he really screwed up."

Reality

"Complex problems take time to resolve. There's no magical solution."

Jealousy

"She has it all."

Fulfillment

"Even though she has different advantages than I, I have my own strengths. Her advantages don't make her better."

Step 2: Review the positive adult replacement.

Once you get used to recognizing when you are making judgments from the child's state, you can train yourself to eliminate judgmental language.

Our language is important. The way we use it reflects our overt and hidden feeling about ourselves and others. If you consciously spend time listening to yourself and others, you're likely to hear many instances of judgmental language. You even hear it when you listen to the news. Make a note of how many times negative labels are applied to describe behavior or explain actions.

Judgmental language always comes from the child's view of the world as dangerous, bad, suspect, and threatening. People don't realize how often it masks reality and prevents options for taking positive actions.

The biggest clue that judgmental language expresses childlike emotions is that it's usually expressed during times of extreme stress.

Think back to a time when you were upset with another

person and you used a judgment to describe the situation. For example, a typical angry encounter between a man and a woman might end with her saying, "You don't care about me. You're so insensitive," while he throws up his hands and says, "I can't deal with you. You're too selfish."

Likewise, a typical angry encounter between a parent and child might have the parent saying, "You're lazy and disobedient. I told you to clean your room an hour ago, and here you are still sitting in front of the TV."

Listen for the judgmental words: insensitive, selfish, lazy, disobedient. Chances are, you can remember a similar situation in your own experience. List the judgmental words that you and another person used to describe each other. Now think about how you might have communicated the same point using different language. Concentrate on avoiding judgmental words and simply expressing what you're really feeling.

Here's an example of the difference, using the same man and woman and parent and child:

Judgmental	*Nonjudgmental*
"You don't care about me. You're so insensitive."	"I don't feel as if you're really listening to me."
"What do you want from me? You're so selfish."	"I don't understand why you're upset."
"You're lazy and disobedient."	"Why haven't you cleaned your room yet?"

When you catch yourself thinking judgmentally (and the words that spring to mind or spring to your lips are often a clue), try to concentrate on stating your concern without negative implications. Ask a question ("Why are you crying?"). Try to listen for the underlying feeling ("She must feel upset"). Give others—and yourself—the benefit of assuming a positive motivation. It will change your language and, consequently, the way you're able to solve problems. Keep in mind that judgmental words push people away—which is not what you intend.

STEP 3: Reshape a positive "match."

Another helpful exercise is called "matching." Matching helps you to see how a person's different style is acceptable. It's an adult way of enhancing closeness and a replacement for the child's symbiosis. Focus on describing the need the behavior is designed to meet, and make a comparison in your own life. Here's a good example of the way matching works. George and Irene, a married couple, were experiencing a basic mismatch that was driving them crazy. George criticized Irene for spending afternoons shopping. Even though she didn't overspend—in fact, most of the time she bought little or nothing—he thought it was frivolous and silly to "waste" the afternoon wandering through shopping malls. I used the matching technique.

First, I asked Irene to describe the kind of pleasure that shopping gave her. She talked about the feeling of freedom, the enjoyment of being away from the responsibilities of home and work—how shopping engaged her on a purely "mindless," sensual level, as she became completely absorbed in colors and textures.

Then I asked George if he could think of any activity that provided him with a similar pleasure. He came up with football games, and told how he was able to "zone out" in front of the TV and become so enraptured with a game that he almost felt as though he were there on the field. He added that Irene often complained when he spent several hours watching a football game.

When Irene and George matched her shopping to his football, they discovered that both activities, although they were different, were aimed at achieving the same positive feelings. Their differences were more stylistic than fundamental. They had nothing to do with goodness or badness.

Defining another's preferences or behavior as good or bad is a sign of the child's simple, rigid view of the world. Rather than create opportunities for sharing, or opening up new vistas, this rigidity builds barriers and closes doors.

In the last chapter, you saw two examples of matching:

1. Rachel and Bob both felt calm when their environment was ordered. Bob's neatness in the physical setting = Rachel's keeping her relationships in order.
2. Laurie and Sam were both upset when their son's girlfriend became pregnant. Laurie's crying = Sam's yelling.

Consider your own situation. Does your partner, friend, or child have a behavior or activity that you think is silly or a problem? Try to find out what that person feels when he or she is doing it. The underlying feeling will give you a clue. The activity might release tension, provide inspiration, or give the person some pleasure. Although it may be a complete mystery to you why anyone would do it, you can probably take the underlying feeling and find a match in something you do. Your ability to match behaviors will help you to become less judgmental.

As an authentic adult, you can appreciate more fully that all humans have fundamental desires and longings. Even when there are differences, our points of similarity are much more profound.

CHAPTER 7

Can You Be an Adult with Your Parents?

- **Are you too strongly influenced by what your parents say?**
- **Do you feel like a child when you're around your parents?**
- **Do you think you can't have a good life until you resolve childhood issues with your parents?**

"My parents can't accept the fact that I'm single," Roberta complained. "They make me feel like a failure." She sat across from me, her face churning with frustration and annoyance.

"What do they do?" I asked.

She grimaced. "They never want to hear about my real life—what's happening at my job, whether I enjoyed my vacation, how I'm feeling. It always comes back to, 'Are you seeing someone?' or, 'Maybe that nice man didn't call you because you were too pushy.' Blah, blah, blah. They're completely unsupportive of me as a single person."

I was curious to meet Roberta's parents and find out what was really going on. I suggested she ask them to come in for a session. She was highly skeptical of this approach, but finally agreed to ask them. "But they probably won't want to come," she warned me. "I don't think they're that concerned with my mental health. They just want me to meet a man."

To Roberta's surprise, her parents were delighted to be asked, and they came with her to her next session. Edna and Walter were a couple in their early seventies, bright-eyed and intelligent, and eager to talk about their daughter. I noticed right away that they adored Roberta. You could see it in their eyes as they looked at her, and when Walter said, "my daughter," his voice carried a ring of pride. All of this escaped Roberta, who sat in a corner of the office looking irritated and uneasy.

I asked Roberta to tell her parents what she had told me. Staring at her lap, she said hesitantly, "I don't feel you accept me because I'm not married. It seems to be the only thing you care about."

Edna and Walter looked at her in surprise. "Oh, honey," Edna said. "Of course we love you just the way you are. It's just that we've been so happy for all these years—we want you to have the same happiness. We never meant to hurt your feelings."

"There are other ways to be happy," Roberta replied. "Besides, you know I'd like to be married. But you make it seem like my fault that the right guy hasn't come along. Your constant harping makes me feel bad."

"I'm sorry," her mother said sincerely. "But you've always said you wanted to get married and have children, so I've tried to help you. And after your father's heart attack, well . . ." her voice trailed off.

"What's that got to do with it?" Roberta asked, shaking her head in dismay. She shot me a look as if to say, 'See, I told you they wouldn't get it.' "

Obviously, Roberta's singleness was a touchy subject. She couldn't hear anything but criticism, although clearly her parents thought they were being loving. They didn't know how to deal with her disappointment about not being married in a way that felt good.

"Roberta," Walter said, clearly uncomfortable with having to put his feelings into words, "I just want you to be taken care of."

"Like I can't take care of myself!" she replied.

"Well, you've had money problems, and we've had to bail you out," he reminded her.

"Your father and I just want you to be happy," Edna said, echoing the sentiments of a million mothers before her.

Roberta bristled against what she perceived to be her parents' lack of support for her choices. It's common to feel criticized or paranoid when you're unhappy. Roberta's pain about being alone was heightened by her parents' reaction. She couldn't recognize their good intentions because she thought they were putting her down. But I could see that Edna and Walter really cared about their daughter, and even admired her. They wanted her to have what she admitted she wanted—as well as what they wanted for her.

I frequently see families who are trapped in the same kind of dilemma. Parents don't know how to express their concerns without sounding critical. Adult children don't know how to stop hearing their parents as omnipotent beings. Roberta was giving Edna and Walter too much power over whether she felt good or bad.

The three of them needed to take two steps before they could settle this issue. First, they had to acknowledge the positive intent in one another's positions. Ironically, Roberta was feeling rejected by her parents and they, in turn, were feeling rejected by her. It was a classic example of a mismatch. But they all cared deeply about one another. As she listened to her parents continue to talk that day about their hopes and desires for her, Roberta began to soften. For the first time, she realized how much they cared. They weren't being unsupportive at all. Just the opposite. "Your parents can't help but worry," I told her. "They've been doing it all your life. They can't automatically switch it off. If you really examine what's going on here, you'll see that you and your parents have a lot of common ground. You want to find a good man to marry, and that's what they want for you. Look at the intent, not the way they express it."

It's the nature of things that children grow up and move away from their parents. They lead different lives because their opportunities and choices are different. Most parents accept, at least rationally, that this is the way it's supposed to be. But many times, both parents and children have trouble actually making the change, and that's why so many adults are still so focused on getting their parents' approval.

THE PARENTAL IMPRINT

We can't really grow up until we stop having childlike responses to our parents—and about that I have bad news and good news. The bad news is that your parents probably didn't have the skills to teach you everything you needed to know about being an adult. The good news is that you can learn what you need to know somewhere else. Even if your childhood was filled with trauma and abuse, you don't have to return there to find the "good" child. You can discover and reclaim your goodness in the interactions you experience as an adult.

When I work with people, I find that they are often eager to talk about the ways their parents have disappointed them, tried to control their lives, or withheld their love. They think they can't get that need met any other way than by working it out with their parents.

Phyllis came to me after she spent years trying to resolve some issues she had with her mother. In the process, the two of them tried everything from throwing pillows to screaming to having long (often accusatory) conversations, to doing "inner child" therapy. You had to give them a great deal of credit for trying, but nothing helped, and Phyllis was at her wit's end. "My mother and I are no closer to resolving our issues than we ever were," she told me miserably.

I knew Phyllis couldn't resolve her issues until she did some adult groundwork and found strength in herself so she could see her parents as flawed, not omnipotent. She felt injured by things that had happened in her childhood. I reminded her of the ways her past therapy had helped, by showing her that it wasn't her fault. But she now had to take the next step, which was to build "corrective" relationships in her current life. I encouraged her to work on the things that were troubling her currently—the problems she was trying to resolve with her husband and children.

Phyllis was baffled. "But what about my mother?" she protested.

I explained to Phyllis that most therapies have been limited because they don't know about E.D. They encourage people to go back and resolve the issues from their childhood so they can function better in their current lives. But it doesn't work. People keep going back, again and again, but what they're looking for isn't there.

I told Phyllis, "You don't have to keep suffering because your mother couldn't provide the things you wanted from her. You won't find them by replaying the past."

I understand why, even as adults, people so often continue to look to their parents as the source of their own failures. After all, when we're children, our parents are our primary role models for how adults are supposed to be. We depend on them to love us and to be our caretakers, and also to teach and guide us in the ways of life. When they fail to perform either of these crucial functions, we assume they acted out of malevolence. Thus, people grow up thinking their parents have deliberately damaged them.

Over the many years that I have been working with people, I've noticed that therapy often helped them to feel validated and to overcome their feelings of unworthiness, whether they'd felt loved by their parents or not. But I've also noticed that when these people confronted new problems that they had difficulty coping with, they would automatically revert to blaming their parents—for example, the woman who claimed that her inability to form stable relationships was directly related to the fact that her mother was emotionally distant.

An entire self-help culture has been erected on the foundation of blaming parents. The internal dialogue goes something like this: "My life is a mess. I can't form relationships. Nothing works. My parents were supposed to teach me how to do it right. That was their job as parents, and they didn't do it."

What most therapies reinforce is the still-present expectation that parents continue to be the sources of our learning about life. When these therapies insist that adults must confront the issues they had with their parents, they assume that people can't possibly find that learning elsewhere. So they keep going back, trying to make peace with the past, as though that will provide the magical solution to the problems they face as adults.

THE MYTH OF PARENTAL OMNIPOTENCE

I have seen that when people begin to learn adult skills on their own and see that their lives are changing, they are able to let go of the painful burden of resenting their parents.

Recently, in my group, two women were talking about their mothers. Mary, an angry young woman in her late twenties, was complaining. "When I visit my mother, she never listens to me. I can be trying to talk about important things, and she's staring out the window. It infuriates me. Her mind is a million miles away. It's been like that all my life. My mother was in her own world and I was invisible. That's what I grew up with."

Joanne, a quiet, rather sweet woman of forty, responded, "I can relate to that. My mother was the same way. I think she was depressed. My father was very critical and domineering. My mother was always cooking and cleaning, obsessively, it seemed. I remember feeling lonely, wanting her to talk to me or listen to what I had to say."

Mary watched Joanne carefully as she was speaking. "There's a softness to your voice," she said, puzzled. "It sounds like you're able to forgive your mother. But I just can't." Her face tightened in determination.

"Well, my mother is quite elderly," Joanne said reflectively. "I want to feel that everything's okay between us before she dies."

"My mother could die tomorrow and it wouldn't change the way I feel," said Mary angrily. "She never cared about me. Why should I care about her?"

As I listened to Mary and Joanne, I found it interesting that these two women, who had objectively similar experiences, could reach such different conclusions. Mary believed that her anger was too big to resolve. It was a signal that she felt hurt, but it kept her a victim. Joanne recognized her mother's failings, but was able to move past them. I thought I knew why.

Joanne and I had been working together for quite a while. Originally, she'd come to me with a relationship problem. She was engaged to marry a man who was very weak and dependent. She was exhausted by the effort of supporting him financially and emotionally. I helped Joanne develop the adult skills she needed to get out of the relationship and begin to pursue the goals she had let fall by the wayside. As her life began to change for the better, Joanne directed less blame at, and felt more compassion toward, her mother. While it was true her mother was unable to hear her, Joanne no longer felt the child's need for complete approval from her parent. Her mother's emotional distance didn't feel like a punishment.

Our parents are not omnipotent, although that's the way we see them when we're children. A child has no way to cognitively grasp what is going on in an adult's life. Here's a simple example that will sound familiar to anyone who's been a parent. You promise your seven-year-old that you'll take her to the park for a picnic the next day, but when you wake up in the morning, it's raining. You say, "I'm sorry, honey, we won't be able to have our picnic today. It's raining." Your daughter wails, "But you promised!" You throw up your hands in frustration. Why can't your daughter see that it's not your fault it rained? You didn't mean to break a promise—it was out of your control. But your daughter is seven years old, and in her mind, it's very straightforward: A promise is a promise. You have all the power. It was your choice—never mind the rain—to not take her on a picnic. Case closed.

Since most parents have emotional dyslexia, they're unable to recognize the child's predictable response, so they get angry. I think of a friend of mine who was complaining about her six-year-old son who had been sick with the flu for three days. She described how exhausted she was the night before after waiting on him hand and foot, bringing him meals, giving him medicine, arranging books and toys on his bed, doing his laundry, and rushing to his room every time he called. At the end of the day, she just wanted him to go to sleep so she could have a minute's peace. But he started begging for a story. "Not tonight," she told him. "Mommy's too tired." His response was to throw his book on the floor and scream, "You're mean!"

When she told me this story, she sighed with defeat. "I felt guilty for saying no to the story, and even guiltier that he thought I was being mean. I was also annoyed that he couldn't see that I had been catering to his every need all day. He should have been able to see how tired I was."

I had to laugh. "He's only six years old," I said. "Six-year-old children don't understand the impact their actions have on others, and they certainly don't think that mothers ever get tired or have any other limits."

My friend's child behaved in an absolutely predictable way for a six-year-old. The problem is, many people carry these ideas about their parents into adulthood. Since their parents were all powerful when they were little, they still allow their parents to be all powerful in their lives.

RE-VIEW YOUR PARENTS

Martin was an energetic, creative man in his mid-thirties who was an executive with a large company. His friends envied his success, but the corporate world made him restless. His dream had always been to be an entrepreneur and start his own company, but his father was vehemently against the idea. "He won't even listen to me," Martin said unhappily. "I told him about this great idea I had for a business, and his instant reaction was, 'Over my dead body will you quit a fine job and get involved in some half-baked scheme.' End of discussion." Martin told me that he was so disheartened by his father's response that he gave up the idea. "But I hate my job. I feel like I'm sleepwalking through life."

My approach with Martin was to do what I call re-viewing—looking at your parents from the perspective of an authentic adult, instead of as the child you were. Using the E.D. Index, I helped Martin see that his reactions to his father were left over from when he was a boy. Even though he was an adult, his response to his father did not reflect the features of the adult state. He had to learn how to be an adult with his father.

"When you thought about approaching your father about this business idea, what were you thinking?" I asked.

Martin rolled his eyes. "That's easy. I had sweaty palms over that. I was thinking, 'He won't like it. He'll think it's a harebrained idea. He'll think I'm being flaky.' "

"Anticipating that reaction must have made you feel stressed," I observed.

He laughed. "No kidding. My father has very definite ideas, and he can turn what seems like a great idea into mush within seconds."

I took the conversation in another direction. "How do you think your father feels about his own career?" I asked.

Martin thought about it for a moment. "It's funny . . . he's never really talked about it. But I suppose he has mixed feelings. He's done okay—worked very hard. I suppose he'd have liked to do better."

"Maybe that's why he's so worried about you," I said. "He wants you to do well."

Martin stiffened. "I can't live out my father's lost dreams," he said.

"No," I agreed. "But as an adult, you can feel empathy for him. It will give you a different way of relating. Right now, you're the scared child with your father. Once you can feel the concern and not the criticism from your father, you can be the powerful adult."

After working with me for several weeks, Martin decided to present his business idea to his father again. Because he could see his father from an adult perspective, he was ready this time to handle his father's concerns directly—to assure him that he had the financial backing and that he'd done his homework. In this conversation, instead of asking his father for approval (which, as an adult, he didn't need), he asked for his help—in the manner of the interdependent adult. His father was still skeptical, but once he saw that Martin was determined to go ahead, with or without his support, he agreed to help. Martin even admitted that his father seemed a little bit flattered that he'd asked him. "He wasn't quite the all-knowing bully I thought he was," he admitted.

One point of struggle between Martin and his father was the fact that sometimes there are "mismatches" between parents and their children. Parents find this very hard to accept. The old boast that, "My son is a chip off the old block," exists more in fantasy than in reality. It's the emotionally dyslexic voice that says your child has to be like you in order for you to be validated.

A great deal of anxiety gets stirred up when a son or daughter rejects the paths his or her parents have chosen. The decision triggers a sense of failure in parents. They wonder, "What's wrong with the way we did it?" Adults with emotional dyslexia have trouble understanding that differences don't have to alienate families. They can strengthen them.

THE POWER OF FORGIVENESS

Amy, age twenty-five, worked for her father in his accounting office. The first time she came to see me, her face was rigid with anger and she was a bundle of nervous tension. As she began to tell me about her father, whom she termed a "brute," her anger only intensified. I listened silently to the cascade of evidence: He was strict at home and very demanding at work. At home, he had always been in charge, but at work he was cold, and she couldn't bear that he treated her like a stranger.

"I can't believe my mother has put up with him all these years," she said. "She never says a word—just takes it. And now, here I am working for him, and I'm right back under his thumb."

Amy believed her father was totally in control, but I

wanted to help her see that his behavior—drinking, yelling, verbal abuse—was a sign that he had no other way to express his needs, fears, and disappointments.

"Do you think your father is happy?" I asked.

"Happy?" She gave me a look that indicated she had never considered it before.

"Usually, when children have temper tantrums, it's because they're unhappy about something. And people who are unhappy don't really have much power." I asked Amy to visualize her father as a little boy throwing a temper tantrum. She looked startled at first, then she laughed, and for the first time, I saw a side of her beyond the anger.

"That's funny," she admitted. "He does look like that when he gets mad."

"Out of control, not powerful," I said. "Recognize the distinction."

I worked with Amy for several weeks, using the E.D. Index to teach her the difference between being powerful and being out of control. As she learned to make distinctions between the child and adult ways of responding, she began to let go of her anger and fear. She lost some of her edginess. Her body language grew softer. Now she was ready to begin observing her father as the human being he was—not as the all-powerful parent who controlled her life and whose approval was a matter of life and death. She conceded that in her anger, she has not given her father credit for the ways he had shown love for her—how he'd always looked out for her, given her business advice, and helped her with her career. And once she recognized that he was not a godlike, malevolent figure, just a struggling unhappy man who loved her in his own way (albeit unsatisfactorily), she was no longer angry with him. More important, she no longer let her feelings about him control her.

Over time, I watched Amy transform herself from a tense, emotionally closed woman to a person with more self-assurance and warmth. She even looked more attractive. Without the weight of her anger, her faced brightened, her shoulders lifted. She was a different woman than the one who had first walked into my office.

Several months after I stopped seeing Amy, I received a surprising phone call from her father. His voice over the phone was gruff, but I could hear that he was a little embarrassed. "I have to meet you," he said. "I have to thank you for giving me back my daughter."

Adult Skill: Forgive Your Parents for Their Past Mistakes

Now that you're an adult, you can let go of your need to make your parents the source of all meaningful approval and learning. That implies acceptance of their humanness, as well as forgiveness for the mistakes they made that still haunt your life.

Relating to your parents as an authentic adult—and therefore forgiving them—is a fundamental skill that will release you from some of the most intense E.D. triggers. There are three steps to this lesson:

1. *Stop* when you feel angry or weak.
2. *Review* your parents' goodness.
3. *Reshape* the way you see your parents.

STEP 1: Stop when you feel angry or resentful.

The secret to forgiving your parents is to learn to see them from the perspective of the adult. That means using your cognitive brain to avoid the child's state. Think about it:

- You can't forgive your parents if you think they are the source of your goodness or badness, or if you believe they have the power to make you feel approved. That is a *dependent* child's reaction.
- You can't forgive your parents if you're still waiting for

them to make your life right. That is a *distorted* child's reaction.

- You can't forgive your parents if you think they can still hurt you or take away from you the things you need. That is a *fearful* child's reaction.

Using the E.D. Index, consider the things your parents have said or done that trigger the child's precognitive emotions in you. Stop and consider how different your reaction might be if you don't react from the knee-jerk child's state. For example:

Child's Emotion	*Adult Response*
"She's so critical."	"She doesn't have another way to express her concern, but I can listen to her intention and hear it as caring."

In this example, the knee-jerk child's response was based on the state of dependency—needing the parent's approval and seeing criticism as an assault on dignity. The adult response of interdependency assumes dignity and allows the listener to hear criticism without feeling assaulted.

STEP 2: Review your parents' goodness.

Parents often have what I call an "intensity gene" when it comes to their children. They are so full of love and concern that sometimes it seems to overflow and encompass them. They worry endlessly about large things and small things, studying their children relentlessly for signs of problems. When you're a child, subject to your parents' devoted scrutiny, it can feel comforting, and also oppressive.

As children mature, they begin to assert their independence. If a mother says, "The one thing you must never do is cross that street alone," the child will become obsessed with crossing the street, not because he wants to be difficult but because he wants to be grown up. As children become older and begin to want more independence, parents get even more worried. By the time children reach their teen years—when they're really asserting their own identities—some parents are beside themselves, especially if they themselves are emotionally dyslexic. They transfer their own fears to their children and view the world as a big, bad place that is booby-trapped for constant danger.

For some parents, the worry never goes away, even after their children are full-grown adults with children of their own. But most people have a hard time seeing that worry as benevolent. Rather, it seems controlling or critical. Begin your lesson by listening to these familiar scenes of conflict between parent and adult child, and observing the positive intent in each one.

Mother: "Have you called the doctor yet?"
INTENT: I'm worried about her. I want her to be okay.
Adult Child: "I think I'm old enough to take care of myself. Stop nagging me."
INTENT: I want her to see me as competent.

Father: "Let me get my mechanic to check that car out before you buy it."
INTENT: I trust my mechanic, and if he says the car is all right, I'll know my son will be safe.
Adult Child: "I can take care of it myself."
INTENT: I'm capable of buying a car on my own.

Mother: "That hairstyle doesn't suit your face."
INTENT: I'm just trying to be helpful.

Adult Child: "You're always so critical!"
INTENT: I want her to accept me as I am.

In each case, the message given and the message received is very different. The parents speak from concern. The children hear criticism. Since people don't know about emotional dyslexia, they don't understand that parents and children, like other humans, sometimes have trouble expressing their good intentions—but they do have them. Only when you have smart emotions can you learn to see your parents' goodness and your own.

Now, think about a similar conflict you have with your own parent. Write a dialogue as shown above. Find the positive intent in your parent's statement, and in your response.

STEP 3: Reshape the way you see your parents.

If you are still struggling with old issues from your childhood, chances are you are operating from the child side. You need to "re-view" your parents from the adult perspective.

Using the E.D. Index, ask yourself these questions about your parents:

Interdependency: Are there ways your parents can help you? Can you ask for that help without feeing dependent on them? Can you define your relationship with your parents in a way that does not blame them or you for things that went wrong? Can you feel worthy without their approval? Can you see them as worthy, even if you don't approve of them?

Awareness: What were your parents' goals in life? What were they trying to achieve beyond their role as parents? Did they have disappointments? Can you see ex-

amples of their good intentions? Now that you're an
adult, can you see things in a larger perspective? As a
child, your parents' actions may have seemed volatile
or overly focused on you. What were the other things
going on in their lives? Describe the circumstances of
your economic and family life as though you were an
outside observer. Can you acknowledge that your parents were never all powerful—that was just the way it
felt as a child? They didn't necessarily know how to
teach you what you needed to learn because they
didn't know how.

Confidence: Can you accept that your parents are not dangerous to you now? Can you separate yourself from the
fear that they can exert negative power over your life?

I have seen the process of re-viewing produce amazing
results—even for people who grew up in abusive homes. Rick,
a young man whose father had often beat him physically,
provided a striking example of the power of adult skills to free
people from being adult victims. When Rick came to see me,
he was full of anger. He wanted revenge on his father. "He
had no right to hit me," he shouted. "What kind of a father is
that? I wanted to confront him with how much he hurt me,
but he died before I had a chance. I hated him. I'll never forget
what he did to me—much less forgive him."

Rick was coiled tight with fury, and although he admitted
that it was interfering with his life, he couldn't get over it. "I
tried all kinds of therapy," he said. "But all it did was prove
that my father was a real bastard."

As Rick told me the brutal stories of his childhood, I could
almost see him transformed into the frightened little boy. I felt
a great deal of sympathy because of the abuse he had suffered. But slowly, I began to draw out the adult in Rick—the
man who could see his father as a weak, humiliated person,
not as an ogre. He began to change his descriptions of him,

talking about his father as a "tragic figure" who was deeply unsatisfied all of his life. "He couldn't do anything right," Rick said sadly. "His business, his marriage, being a father. He was a mess. Unfortunately, I was his victim."

My approach with Rick was not to work on his relationship with his father, but to work on achieving adult skills in his life. Previous therapy had focused on the relationship, but without the skills, it didn't work. One day, about eight months after we started, Rick called me on the phone to tell me about a startling flash he'd had that morning. "I was shaving," he said in a voice filled with awe. "And suddenly, I looked in the mirror and saw my father's face. I never realized before how much I looked like him! I was stunned. I stood there frozen for about five minutes, and . . . well, I realized I liked that face. I . . . [here his voice broke] I liked that face. My father's face." He was so moved by his discovery that he couldn't go on.

It was a big breakthrough for Rick. For a moment in time, he had recognized something he liked in his father's face, which was now his face. Finally, he was ready to move on.

When you stop being a child with your parents, you have learned an important lesson in being an authentic adult. It will transform not only your relationship with your parents but your other relationships as well.

CHAPTER 8

Can You Raise E.D.-free Kids?

- **Is your home a battleground?**
- **Does being a parent trigger the child in you?**
- **Do you sometimes wonder if you're a good parent?**

If you're around children a lot, it's not always so easy to resist getting angry and losing your control when they whine, cry, get sassy, or behave in otherwise obnoxious ways. Most parents feel guilty when they blow up at a kid, no matter how badly he's behaving, because it makes them feel too much like children themselves. To be sure, it's normal enough for parents to sometimes feel angry, confused, or frustrated with their children. But when those feelings trigger the child states, they interfere with the primary role of parents—which is to love and to teach. Learning to relate positively to children will help you whether you have children of your own or not.

Most of us were raised by parents with emotional dyslexia, who passed it on to us. If as children we heard that we were bad, lazy, or hopeless, those were the messages we believed. Remember, children see their parents as omnipotent and they assume that what a parent says is true. As a result, our emotional memories trigger negative feelings. Unless children learn differently, those negative messages will not get transformed into positive messages in adulthood.

One of the most important things parents can do is teach their children replacement behavior as their cognitive skills develop. That's what I try to do with the children in my life. Here's one example.

My friend's ten-year-old son could be a real handful. When he got worked up about something, he was obnoxious and disruptive, and he'd drive everyone crazy. His biggest problem was that when he was frustrated or disappointed, he started screaming. I noticed that the adults around him usually reacted by either yelling at him or sending him to his room.

I spent a lot of time with this boy. It was obvious that he didn't enjoy his tantrums any more than the people around him. On some level, he had to be aware of how ineffective his tantrums were because they usually resulted in punishment instead of getting him what he wanted. But he didn't seem to know how to stop them.

One day, he was visiting me and he wanted to eat some candy. When I said no, because we were getting ready to eat dinner, he started screaming. I pointedly ignored his tantrum, and I decided to try a different approach. Later that night, when he was calm, I sat him down for a talk.

"When you couldn't have that candy today, you started screaming, and it didn't help much, did it?" I asked.

He shook his head no and stared at his feet.

"You didn't get the candy, did you?"

"No."

"What usually happens when you scream?"

He shrugged. "Oh, my parents yell at me and send me to my room."

"I see. So, when you scream, you usually get punished, plus you don't get what you want. Boy, I guess screaming doesn't work very well, does it?"

He looked up at me and said "No . . ." Then he added in a small voice, "I don't want to scream, but I don't always know when it's going to happen."

Exactly, I thought. This child had inadvertently articulated the precise way children feel most of the time—as though they have no control over what happens to them, and no control over their dramatic responses. He was just as frustrated as everyone else that he couldn't control his screaming.

Since he was a bright child who enjoyed a challenge, I decided to try an experiment with him while he was visiting me. "Let's do this," I suggested. "When I think you're starting to get upset about something, I'll say 'S.' That will be our secret code that means 'Stop.' No one else will know about it but you and me. When I say 'S,' it will be a signal for you to stop what you're doing and count to ten. Then you can say what's on your mind."

He agreed eagerly. It sounded like a game to him—a game that would make him feel better by giving him more control.

The next day, as I was preparing dinner, he came into the kitchen. "Let's practice saying 'S,' " he said. He wasn't upset about anything, so I didn't understand at first why he wanted to practice. Then I realized that he had already figured out that he needed to learn how to respond to my 'S' signal when he was calm so he'd have the knack of it when he was feeling stressed. The practice was like building a pathway to his cognitive brain.

I was touched to see how much he wanted to have more control of himself, and to learn how to react to being upset without screaming. I looked at his hopeful little face and thought of how easily and wrongly we adults slip into the thinking that some children are bad because their behavior is annoying. Here before me was a perfect example of how recognizing a child's positive intent revealed his willingness to do better. He was motivated to learn, and we practiced until he could count to ten without moving his lips. He even asked me to teach his mom and dad, and they used the "S," too. Before long, he had learned to recognize the signals on his own. He started calling his own "stops," and his whole demeanor changed. That's an example of emotional learning.

As you know, ten-year-old boys are not prone to open displays of affection, but for my birthday that year he picked out a card that showed two people kissing. I was moved to tears by the card. It felt so wonderful to know I'd made an impact on this child's life by focusing on his goodness.

TRANSFORMING THE "BAD" CHILD

One of the hardest things for adults to deal with is seeing their child fall into a chronic pattern of dishonest behavior—for example, not doing homework and lying about it, or stealing candy from the store. When confronted with this behavior, parents often fall into a mixed bag of childlike responses:

- "What's wrong with me as a parent?" (Shame, stemming from feelings of helplessness, because their child has a problem and it reflects upon their competence as parents.)
- "How could my child do this to me?" (Egocentricity, stemming from the distorted feeling that everything your child does is directed at you.)
- "He can't do anything right." (Rigidity, stemming from the fear that your child will fail in life.)

They're angry or frightened because their child is being dishonest, and that's a normal reaction. Parents know it is their responsibility to protect their children from developing troublesome behavior. But the feelings of responsibility coupled with E.D. can bog them down and interfere with their ability to help their children learn different ways of handling their fear or humiliation.

Often, parents get so upset about this behavior that they overreact, without realizing that their child is upset, too. But in fact, the child's own discomfort about his behavior is the key to changing it. Nobody enjoys being a sneak. If you think back to a time when you were dishonest or told a lie (most people have!), try to remember how it felt. Probably, it felt lousy. No one likes to be branded a liar, and kids don't like this behavior any more than adults do. It doesn't feel comfortable. So a child wouldn't deliberately do something that made him uncomfortable without there being an underlying reason. The adult's job is to find out what the reason is and use it to help him.

I once worked with a woman whose twelve-year-old son lied about a failing mark he got on a test. She found the test paper crumpled in a ball at the bottom of his book bag, and she was furious. She immediately marched into his room and confronted him. "Why did you lie to me?" she yelled. "You said you got a B on this test, and look, here it is. You got an F. What's wrong with you?"

She admitted to me later how guilty she felt about screaming at her son, who cowered in a corner of his room, looking miserable and trapped. "I was so mad," she said, "and I hated the way I sounded. But on the other hand, I have no idea how I might have handled the situation differently. He lied to me, plus he flunked the test. It would have been wrong to coddle him or ignore it."

I asked her, "Why do you think he lied to you?"

"Obviously, so he wouldn't get in trouble."

"Exactly," I said. "He lied to you because he was afraid, not because he was bad. If you see him as afraid, not bad, it changes your whole reaction."

I suggested another way she might have responded. "You knew he was hiding his test from you because he was afraid of how you would react. Remember, your intention as a parent isn't to punish him but to help him find a way to do better in school. What if you had said this to him: 'You must have been scared that I'd find out about the test. Were you afraid that your teacher was going to call me?' Now you've created a connection between you and him. He knows you understand how he feels, so maybe he won't need to be so deceptive. Then talk to him about why he flunked the test—he didn't understand the material, he stayed up too late, he didn't study, he was worried about something and got distracted. When you label your kid as bad, you close off the options to help him change his behavior. If you engage him in helping you find a solution, you'll get better results."

The same approach worked when a friend discovered that her young daughter was secretly walking to the store to buy candy with the change left over from groceries. Instead of getting angry, my friend tried another approach. She asked her daughter how it felt when she sneaked off by herself to buy candy. The girl said it made her feel grown up at first because she could walk into the store and get what she wanted. By the time she got home she felt guilty. She added that her mother didn't understand what it felt like to be a kid in New York City and not be able to go places on her own. "I always have to be with you," she complained.

My friend was worried about her daughter going out alone, because the city could be a dangerous place for a child. At the same time, she understood her daughter's need to feel some independence, and wanted to give it to her without her daughter having to sneak change from her mother's purse and feeling bad about herself. Buying candy at the store had become a symbol of freedom for the girl. My friend began to allow her daughter more mobility, give her more allowance, and let her visit friends during the day. Her daughter stopped taking change for candy because she didn't need to anymore. Again, by recognizing a positive intent—the desire for freedom—my friend and her daughter were able to solve the problem. When children sense that you respect their needs, instead of thinking that they're bad, they feel loved and are more willing to cooperate with problem solving.

When you assume a positive motivation for a child's problem behavior, it relieves both you and your child. Instead of being a disciplinarian—a role no parent really enjoys—you have an opportunity to teach your child to solve problems in a way that enhances his or her self-esteem.

I once worked with a woman who suffered throughout her childhood because she had a learning disability that was never diagnosed. Her parents were constantly saying, "What's wrong with you? You're so smart—how could you bring home these grades?" Everyone always assumed that she wasn't trying hard enough. That was the only explanation. Her parents weren't mean; they just didn't have access to another explanation for her poor grades. They believed that when a smart kid fails it's because she's not studying. This woman grew up thinking that she was lazy, because she had heard it so often. When she found out in adulthood that she had a learning disability, a tremendous weight was lifted from her shoulders. She didn't have to be bad or lazy anymore. She just needed a different kind of help.

When she told me about the agonies she had suffered as a child, she was filled with rage at her parents. "They destroyed my self-esteem. How could they do that? What lousy parents!"

I let her express her anger. It helped her move away from feeling that it was somehow her fault. Then I tried to help her see that her parents weren't bad people any more than she had been a bad child. They didn't know she had a learning disability; people didn't understand then what we know today about that problem. And because they had emotional dyslexia themselves, there was no explanation for a smart child doing poorly other than that she was lazy. She eventually learned to forgive her parents because she realized that they didn't know better.

Most of us were raised by parents who loved us and took care of us in the best way they knew how. If we understand that they did not necessarily have adult skills to help them, we can stop blaming them for the ways they failed.

CHILDREN RAISED BY CHILDREN

Because we love our children, they are the receptacles of our greatest expectations. Part of that is legitimate worry. Parents naturally want their children to be educated, to receive the tools to make it in the world. But if we bring to their training our own childlike thinking—and our accompanying melodramatic reactions—we are hampered from helping them grow up to be real adults.

Let's examine the different ways a parent might react to the common circumstances of raising a child—first from the point of emotional dyslexia, then from the perspective of the authentic adult. As you know from doing the lessons, you get from one to the other by engaging your cognitive thinking before you react to a problem.

Your child fails in school:

Emotionally Dyslexic Adult	*Authentic Adult*
You fear your child will never make it. You imagine him in the future as a bum. You threaten to punish him if he fails again.	You're concerned that something is interfering with your child's learning, and you try to find out what it is. You understand that problems are correctable, and you calmly enlist the help of others to create solutions.

Your son gets into a fight at the playground:

Emotionally Dyslexic Adult	*Authentic Adult*
You overreact and blame the child of his friends. You worry that your child might get beat up or be a bully.	You know little boys sometimes get overly rambunctious on the playground as a way of letting off steam, and it's usually not dangerous. You let the boy explain what happened, and offer alternative responses to hitting when he has a conflict.

Mothers sometimes have a hard time seeing that little boys use aggressive behavior to let off steam. It's part of the natural way they express themselves. Mothers get scared that their boys are becoming violent or learning destructive impulses. But, as we discussed with adult men, aggressive behavior is partially hormonal. It is the parents' role to help boys express aggression positively—not to force them to stop being boys. That's impossible. I think of the friend who wouldn't allow any toy guns in her house. Her boy went out into the yard and fashioned a gun from a tree branch. I'm not suggesting that guns and violence are okay. But parents have to understand that they can't help a child learn if they begin with a rigid premise that "what you want to do is bad." The irony is, if you're overly afraid of their aggressiveness, you'll make them feel bad about themselves and they'll become more aggressive.

Your child acts sassy and disobeys you:

Emotionally Dyslexic Adult	*Authentic Adult*
You go nuclear and attack the child. You yell, "You have a foul mouth," or, "No child of mine speaks to his parent that	You know that a parent's role is to teach a child why certain behaviors are unacceptable, while being a role model your-

way!" Or you ignore their behavior because you're afraid of
conflict.

self. You also know it's easier
to teach when you're not in
E.D. yourself. You try to see
the positive intent behind the
child's sassiness, and use this
connection to transform her
behavior.

Your daughter wears too much makeup:

Emotionally Dyslexic Adult

You worry that your daughter
is growing up too fast. You get
alarmed and grow disgusted.
You snap, "You look like a
slut! No daughter of mine will
leave the house looking like
that!" You drag her into the
bathroom and make her wash
all the makeup off her face.

Authentic Adult

You look for the positive intent
behind wearing too much
makeup. She wants to look
pretty, feel grown up, be like
her peers. You sympathize
with her because you know
how much ambivalence she
has about growing up, and
how hard it is to do. You
might still make her wash her
face, but your attitude would
be one of compassion, not disgust. You try to help her understand that her behavior and
appearance have an impact.

Every generation of parents and children faces the inevitable opposition about appearance. Teenagers assert their independence by adopting styles that are in conflict with their
parents' tastes. It's the most predictable thing in the world.
You might be horrified when your daughter shaves one side
of her head, or your son has his ear pierced, but it will help to
remember how you once asserted yourself in exactly the same
way. Kids have so little power over their lives; appearance is
one area where they feel some control. As one man said,
shaking his head with the irony, "When I was young, I grew

my hair long, and my parents went ballistic. They thought it was the ultimate evil. Now my son shaved his hair off, and I found myself reacting exactly the same way. After I calmed down, I couldn't escape the humor of it."

Your child steals candy from a store:

Emotionally Dyslexic Adult	*Authentic Adult*
You're humiliated that your child would steal. You express disgust and fury: "How could you do this to me? You're no good."	You help your child see that although his intentions are positive, his actions may have a negative impact. You ask the child why he was stealing and try to find the positive intent behind the action. As a role model, you teach the child that actions have consequences and his behavior has an impact. For instance, you arrange with him to do chores to earn and repay what the candy cost.

Your son acts embarrassed to be seen with his mother:

Emotionally Dyslexic Adult	*Authentic Adult*
You're hurt. You say, "What's wrong with you? Don't you love me? Why do you care so much about what your friends think?"	You understand the child's need for autonomy—to seem older and more independent. You also know that young boys are sensitive to being labeled as sissies if they're too close to their mothers. You know better than to take it as a personal condemnation.

Your teenager is aloof and won't talk to you:

Emotionally Dyslexic Adult	Authentic Adult
You fear that she's hiding something important, and you panic. You feel cut off and rejected. You resent her for shutting you out.	You evaluate her overall behavior and decide if you really have reason to be concerned about drugs or other serious issues. You understand that teenagers need privacy, and don't want to share as much. This is normal. You also get support from other parents because the withdrawal and criticism from teens can be painful.

Parents with teenagers sometimes feel that they can't win. They know a teen demands and needs some independence, but they're also aware of all the dangers lurking in their child's path. The desire to protect and the need to let go seem in direct conflict. That's why life with a teenager can sometimes turn into a battle zone. Parents need to recognize the distinction between behavior that is dangerous—such as taking drugs or drinking—and behavior that is simply obnoxious. Withdrawing, criticizing, and challenging your values are normal forms of separation. These behaviors feel hurtful and insulting at the time, but as an adult you can view them in perspective—even remembering how you behaved in similar ways when you were a teenager.

For most of your teen's life, you have been all powerful. Now the teen must find his own power—something that comes from himself, not from you. But because he's not confident, he expresses his way by criticizing yours—saying, for instance, "I'd never have your lifestyle," or, "My values are better than yours."

It's an awful time for parents who feel that they've given so much love and support, only to be slapped in the face. They think, "I don't deserve this. Why is he doing this to me?" If parents step away from the automatic reflex of "he's doing this to hurt me," they can see that the teenager's criticism isn't directed at them. He's doing it for himself, to try to form an identity that is distinct from yours. By the time your child is a teenager, he knows he has to leave you soon. That's frightening. So he puffs himself up with false bravado and tells you he knows better than you do. As an adult, you have the ability to listen to the discomfort behind his hurtful words and withdrawal, and see it as a normal process, not deliberately vindictive behavior.

When circumstances arise that demand you take a firm position that goes against what your child wants, you can be firm without causing humiliation. I'm not recommending a permissive attitude. Your responsibilities are real and weighty. But if you understand what your child is feeling, you can respond more lovingly while still making tough decisions. For example, your daughter may regard your refusal to let her go to a late-night concert as a sign that you don't trust her. She hears the message, "You think I'm going to do something bad." As a parent, you can take responsibility for your child's safety without turning it into a judgment. You might say, "I know my decision seems wrong to you, and I'm sorry. But I'm concerned about you. I trust you, but I know there are people who can't be trusted, and it's my job to protect you from them."

Your child doesn't want to go to college:

Emotionally Dyslexic Adult	*Authentic Adult*
You're horrified. You tell him that you know what's best, and he'll do what you tell him.	You ask him what he wants to do. Find out what his interests are, and examine the options

You express fear that he'll
never amount to anything.

for meeting those interests.
Also determine whether he's
rejecting college out of fear or
because he has a real desire to
do something different. If it's
fear, you can help him see the
experience in a more positive
light.

I know a couple who struggled with their son over this
issue. He was an extremely bright boy who always got good
grades in school, and they were very proud of him. When he
announced, halfway through his senior year of high school,
that he didn't want to go to college, they were stunned. Both
of them had master's degrees, and they valued higher education. It had never occurred to them that their son wouldn't go
to college.

Weeks of anger, tears, and pressure followed the boy's
announcement. His mother tried to convince him to change
his mind. His father withdrew and became silent. He refused
to discuss it at all. When they finally came to me with their
problem, the family was at an impasse.

From the parents' viewpoint, it was very clear-cut: "If Ted
doesn't go to college, all he has to look forward to is a life of
crummy, low-paying jobs. We didn't raise him to be a short-
order cook in a diner."

I knew these were very loving parents, and they only
wanted what was best for their son. But emotional dyslexia
was keeping them from seeing the total picture. They were
making a rigid judgment: If Ted didn't go to college, he would
have a lousy life. There was no other possibility. They were
lacking perspective: If Ted didn't go to college now, his entire
life would be ruined. He would never have the opportunity
again.

They were so certain of their position that they hadn't

really been listening to Ted. What was he feeling? What was his positive intent in not wanting to go to college?

I met with Ted alone, and started to explore the issue with him. I didn't open the session with the question, "Why don't you want to go to college?" That would have sounded like an accusation, and he would have been put on the defensive. Instead, I asked him to tell me about his interests and about the things he enjoyed doing. He grew animated as he talked about his love of science, particularly archaeology. And he added that he also enjoyed art and photography. "There are so many things I like," he said. "I just don't know what I want to be."

I asked him why he had to decide right now, and he rolled his eyes. "You know how it is. Everyone pushes you to say what you're going to major in and what you're going to do with the rest of your life. My parents have successful careers, and I know they expect a lot out of me. But I just don't know what I want to do. I'm afraid of disappointing them. What if I hate college? What if I can't decide what I want to do?"

My conversation with Ted revealed that he was afraid of taking the big step into adulthood that college represented. Because he was young, he had no perspective. He had no way of knowing that whatever happened during his first year of college, it wouldn't make or break the rest of his life. Inadvertently, his high school teachers and his parents had set him up to believe that any decision he made now would be a matter of life or death. No wonder he was scared!

I tried to help Ted and his parents view the situation more expansively. I suggested to his parents that if Ted chose to do something else for a year or two, then go to college, that wouldn't be the end of the world. I encouraged them to look at options. I also suggested that they find ways to reassure their son that he shouldn't be afraid of failing. Even if he went to college and struggled during his first year, it would be a valuable learning experience.

I told Ted the same thing. "The nice thing about college is that it opens you up to meeting different people and hearing many viewpoints. You might discover ways to fulfill your interests that surprise you. What's the worst thing that could happen?"

"I could flunk," he replied. "I'd hate for my parents to spend all that money and then disappoint them by failing."

"I can really understand your anxiety," I said. "It's scary to go into a situation that is foreign to you, and not know whether you can do it or not. Your mind is jumping ahead and making all kinds of assumptions based on the terrible things that might happen. You probably felt the same way when you started high school."

He laughed. "Oh, yeah. My freshman year was a bitch."

"But you made friends, and got involved, and it all worked out."

"That's true," he nodded. "I didn't think of that."

"You can use the memory of your past experience to make the future seem less frightening," I told him. "You also know that if you start to feel like you're getting into trouble, you can tell your parents or come to me, and we'll help you. Nobody expects you to handle this alone."

Once Ted understood that college wasn't dangerous—that he could attend in a spirit of openness and exploration—he began to feel less threatened by the idea. He could view it as one more step in life's learning process, not as a do-or-die endeavor.

Parents also need to remember, as we discussed in the last chapter, that sometimes there are real mismatches between themselves and their children. You might see a college education as the ticket to a happy future, but your child may view happiness as being a chef in a restaurant, and not necessarily pursuing a higher education. Or you might have trouble understanding why your daughter doesn't want children; she sees her future a different way than you saw yours. You can't assume that your children will find gratification, happiness, or success by following your path.

EXPANDING THE CHILD'S WORLD

Parents often make the mistake of thinking their children view life from basically the same reference point as adults do. But a child's emotional world is completely different. For example, observe the way a three-year-old behaves when her parents bring home a new baby home from the hospital. She might act angry and aggressive, fearful that she might be supplanted in her parents' affections by this strange interloper. Loving parents will often try to address the child's fears openly—such as by saying, "We love you so much, we decided to have another baby." They think they're being comforting, but a three-year-old child does not have the rational equipment to see the point. As one child psychologist described it, "It's like telling your wife, I love you so much I've decided to get another wife."

A child's greatest dilemma is how to interact in a world that seems totally out of his control. Everything that occurs seems like it's being done to him. His parents can have another baby, decide what to eat for dinner, move to a new house, and choose whether or not to take him to the circus— and he's ultimately helpless to control any of it. If you listen to the emotions being expressed behind a child's temper tantrum, you often see that the child who cries "No!" or angrily informs you that "You're not the boss" is desperately trying to gain control in an environment where he often feels he has none.

You can also avoid making provocative statements that are quite ridiculous when you understand a child's world.

Think about how often you have said or heard other parents say things like, "Don't be such a baby" (but the child is a "baby," at least emotionally). Or "Use your head" (but the child doesn't have the cognitive skills to figure things out on his own). Or "Grow up" (he can't do it by himself). These are pretty confusing messages for kids who have essentially no tools to do what has been asked of them.

You can help your child grow emotionally by first affirming his basic goodness, and then by giving him replacement ways to express his feelings. In the following lesson, I will teach you the skills of being an authentic adult with your children—and in the process, helping them to grow up, too. When you're an adult role model, you'll make your children feel safer in the moment. You also give them the positive message that they too can someday learn this empowering behavior.

Adult Skill: Be an Adult with Your Children

The primary thing that distinguishes an adult from a child is that an adult has the tools of cognitive thinking to help relate to the world and solve problems. If you are reacting to your child from the child's state yourself, you'll find that your household is chaotic—a constant battleground of children vying to have their needs met.

As an adult, you can avoid reacting from dependency, distortion, and fear. And better still, you can teach your children to integrate cognition to solve their problems. This is the missing link in your own life. Because your parents had E.D. themselves, you were never taught how to transform your reactions during stress. If you teach skills to your children, they will take those skills into adulthood. Stress won't automatically trigger precognitive emotions because they will have learned adult replacements.

Parents have two primary roles—to love and to teach. These roles are the basis of the three steps in this lesson:

1. *Stop* before you react in anger.
2. *Review* why your child reacts childishly.
3. *Reshape* your child's behavior.

STEP 1: Stop before you react in anger.

I often talk to parents who basically feel like children themselves, because when their kids do something provocative—screaming in the supermarket, nagging, mouthing off in a sassy tone—it triggers their precognitive emotions. They blow up, punish the child, then later feel deeply guilty. People say to me with great concern, "I know that a good parent doesn't react that way, but I just can't help myself."

First, I assure them that they're not bad parents. That's emotional dyslexia talking. Everyone feels angry sometimes, and parents can become so intensely focused on their children that they don't know any other way to react. The problem isn't that they feel annoyed or even angry. The issue is how they express their anger. Sometimes, it's just impossible to avoid the rush of strong feelings, but your intensity should be a red flag that warns you to pause before you proceed, to avoid being in the child state. Taking a time-out helps you engage your cognitive thinking, and in the process it helps your child learn to do the same.

Let's take an example that every parent can understand to show how time-out can be a useful tool. Your six-year-old daughter wants to go to the park and play on the swings. You just got home from work, and you're exhausted. All you want is to put your feet up and do nothing.

CHILD: "Let's go, let's go."
PARENT: "Not right now, honey. Mommy's tired."
CHILD: "Oh, please, please. I want to play outside."

(The parent thinks, Is she deaf? I said I was tired.)

PARENT: "I said, not today. Maybe tomorrow."
CHILD: "But I want to go now. Take me now!" (She starts to cry.)

(The child thinks, She's mean. She would take me to the park if she was a nice mommy. The child doesn't grasp the concept of mommy being tired.)

PARENT: "No! Don't be so selfish! Get out of my sight and go to your room!"
CHILD: "You're mean! I hate you!" (Runs crying from the room.)

(Parent collapses in a chair, feeling angry and guilty.)

This parent assumed that her daughter had the cognitive ability to understand and sympathize with her mother's tiredness. But you can't expect children to automatically employ adult reasoning. Children are fundamentally egocentric. They believe that if you don't meet their needs, it's because you don't want to. They hear the message that their needs are bad.

It would have helped if this parent had stopped herself before her anger became too great, and tried to relate to her child's positive intent. When her child started to cry, it was a signal that things were turning explosive. At that point, she might have said, "Boy, you're full of energy today. Why don't you do your cartwheels for Mommy while I sit here and watch."

If you affirm your child's positive intent, it can help defuse the upset. It doesn't mean that you and your children won't have conflicts. You can even let your child know that it's okay to feel angry. But communicate that it's easier to hear what she's saying when she's not being fresh or yelling.

Step 2: Review why your child reacts childishly.

You can only love your child from the adult state, where interdependency, awareness, and confidence govern. The first step is to practice observing your child's actions from an adult perspective. Consider your child's reactions through the screen of the E.D. Index. Remember, a child really *does* live in the child's state! If you acknowledge that, you'll have an eas-

ier time being compassionate, even when your child misbe-
haves. That, in turn, will help you remain in an adult state
yourself.

For one week, make a note of every time your child does
something that upsets you. Write down the incident and your
response. For example:

Incident: He tracked mud on the floor.
Reaction: He doesn't care that I just mopped the floor.

Incident: She was sassy.
Reaction: She hurt my feelings.

Now, use the E.D. Index to find replacement responses
that reflect an understanding of the child's needs. One clue is
that you are avoiding making negative judgments about the
child. For example:

Incident: He tracked mud on the floor.
Positive Intent: Mud is fun.
Adult Response: Explain that mud is fun but it belongs
 outside. It's not so much fun in the house because
 mom has to clean it up. Enlist the child to help clean
 the floor. In this way, you avoid making a negative
 judgment, and teach the child that his actions have
 consequences.

Incident: She was sassy.
Positive Intent: She wanted to go out with her friends
 and you said no.
Adult Response: Understand that the child's reaction is a
 sign that she is feeling upset or stressed. Find the intent beneath the hurtful words. Offer compassion instead of judgment, such as, "I know you want to be
 with your friends, and you're angry with me because I

need you here." In this way, you let the child know that her words were inappropriate, while offering compassion.

I'm not suggesting that you should be wishy-washy with your children. As an adult, you must make rules and set guidelines for behavior. But if you stay in the adult mode, you'll be able to have a positive impact on your children and solve problems as they arise so they don't become unmanageable. Practice this step whenever your child says or does something that triggers childlike emotions in you.

STEP 3: **Reshape your child's behavior.**

There is no such thing as a bad child. Just as adults have positive motivations, even when they behave ineffectively, children are always striving to be the best they can be. The problem is, a child's world is very dramatic because he lacks cognitive skills. If you look at the child's side of the E.D. Index, you'll find a description of the world a child lives in all the time:

1. *Dependency:* He can't take care of himself. He can't build his own self-esteem. All of his signals come from others.
2. *Distortion:* All your actions seem focused on him. When things go wrong, he feels it's his fault.
3. *Fear:* He is completely vulnerable, so life feels dangerous.

You reinforce the precognitive emotions by telling a child he's bad or worthless, by not encouraging him to know that others have needs, and by behaving like a child yourself—thus depriving him of the safety of having an adult to guide him.

Practice reshaping your child's behavior in a positive way, using the E.D. Index. You can help your child begin the process of learning adult skills, even when he is very young.

Sometimes the most effective way to help a child through a crisis is to affirm his experience. That doesn't mean trying to give reasonable explanations. Most of the upset children express stems from their fear that no one is paying attention to what they need. For example:

> **Situation:** Your child is angry because he didn't get as many cookies as his sister. He comes to you sobbing, "Sally got three and I only got two. It's not fair!"
>
> **The adult acting as a child responds:** "Life isn't fair, and that's that. Don't bother me about such a stupid thing."
>
> **The adult teacher responds:** "I know it doesn't seem fair that Sally got three cookies and you only got two. I'm sorry you feel bad. Come here—let me give you a hug. Maybe we could play with your toy racing cars."

In this example, the "adult teacher" is affirming the child's experience, which comes from *egocentricity*. At the same time, she is teaching the child *empathy* by asking for his help.

> **Situation:** It's bedtime and your child is begging and nagging you to let her stay up longer.
>
> **The adult acting like a child responds:** "If you ask me one more time, I'll send you to bed without a story."
>
> **The adult teacher responds:** "It must seem like a fun idea to stay up late. That's funny because sometimes I wish I could go to bed early. I'll tell you what. On Saturday, you can stay up until 9:30."

In this example, the "adult teacher" understands that her daughter, who operates in a state of *fantasy*, really does believe it's glamorous to stay up late. She affirms her daughter's *fantasy*, while playfully suggesting the *reality*.

> As an adult, you have the opportunity to use your cognitive brain to resolve differences with your children to help them, too. You can transform your emotional dyslexia and be a role model of adult behavior. The impact of that learning will enable your child to learn the skills needed to grow up to be a real adult, too. It's the best gift you could give to a child!

CHAPTER 9

Can You Have Power in the World?

- Do you worry that you're not as attractive, interesting, or capable as other people?
- Do you think people will find you too needy or weak if you ask for help?
- Do you expect to be put down or rejected?

Craig came to see me because he had lost his job and was having trouble getting his act together to go on job interviews. Although the reason he was laid off had nothing to do with his abilities (his entire division was eliminated in a corporate restructuring), he was full of self-doubt. The stress of losing his job had triggered precognitive reactions of dependency, distortion, and fear. He couldn't shake the feeling that this was a personal failure—that he might have done something differently to keep his job. He was used to being strong, independent, and full of self-worth. He wasn't used to asking for help or being vulnerable. "I don't feel like myself anymore," he told me. "I can't sleep. I wake up in a panic. I've interviewed for jobs before, and I've never felt this way." Craig's experience was one of having "lost" himself. Where was that confident guy he used to be? In a sense, he had lost himself because the precognitive emotions he was feeling left him without the resources he'd come to rely upon.

As we talked about his past experience, I learned that Craig had changed jobs several times, but always by choice. He had pursued other jobs from a position of security. He didn't need to change; he wanted to—to earn more money or to find something more challenging. A couple of times, he was pursued when he wasn't even looking. "In the past, I even had fun going on job interviews," he said wryly. "I enjoyed presenting myself to people and answering their questions. But now, I just break into a cold sweat thinking about it."

Craig was completely baffled. How could he have suddenly gone from being a self-confident, competent executive to being an anxiety-ridden, frightened person? Could he get his confidence back? My goal was to show Craig that he could experience stress and still be an adult—that adults sometimes do feel anxious and need special help, but this doesn't make them weak or unworthy. However, Craig was battling cultural as well as personal demons. I knew it was common for men to feel this way when they lost their jobs regardless of the circumstances. The most vivid example of that appeared in Studs Terkel's book, *Hard Times*. Terkel was amazed to find that the men he interviewed about the experience of being jobless during the Depression blamed themselves. Clearly, these individuals weren't to blame for the greatest economic catastrophe to hit the nation in this century. But they accepted personal blame for conditions that were outside their control.

I reminded Craig that in the past making a change had always been his decision. Now, it wasn't his choice, so it felt a lot like being a child without control. "Because stress makes you feel weak, it becomes a trigger and you're flooded with childlike memories of what you felt like when you *were* weak," I said. "The stress of having an uncertain future has caused you to lose touch with your adult self, and that's normal, under the circumstances. But we can work to keep you in touch. When you experience stress as an adult, you can feel worried without feeling flawed."

I asked Craig to begin by recalling some of his past experiences with job interviews. "Step outside of yourself and watch yourself in those interviews, as if you were watching a movie. What do you see?"

He closed his eyes and contemplated for a moment. "I see an affable guy, smart, at ease. He's smiling at the man behind the desk." Craig opened his eyes. "That's the guy I used to be. I was a real go-getter. I remember, even when I didn't get a job I interviewed for, I always left knowing I'd made a good impression. In those days, people would say things like, 'Oh, I've heard great things about you.' "

As he began to remember, I noticed that Craig's face was coming to life for the first time since he'd sat down in my office. I began to observe a different man than the defeated, frightened one who had first walked in. Now I, as an observer, could see something of the reasons for Craig's previous success.

"You're still that person," I said. "Objectively, nothing has changed to suddenly make you someone else. But let's be frank. If you're like most men, you have probably spent your life thinking you always had to be a winner at work and can only feel validated if you're successful. You've never had the experience of being outside the loop, so you automatically react with shame. You think you can't hold your head up because you're not, at this moment, being that successful guy."

I assured him that I wasn't looking for a superhuman response. "In fact," I told him, "when you're under stress you probably need more help in order to keep your worries based in reality. If you let being laid off drive you into a feeling of shame, it's going to make things harder. We have to help you stay that smart, confident man you described to me in the 'movie,' because as you've seen in the past, that's the guy people want to hire, and that's the guy you really want to be. If you approach job hunting from the state of shame or neediness, it will be harder for you to perform in interviews."

Craig seemed to grasp my point, and he looked a little more hopeful. The next step was to reconnect him to his skills. Fear had driven away his memory of how good he was at his job, and I knew from my own experience and recent studies of out-placement centers that the people who did best in Craig's position stayed focused on their skills rather than on their previous position or image. I had to get Craig to think about what he could do—to find a balance between his successful past and the current reality of his being out of work. I asked him to do some homework before our next session. "Write down the reasons you were chosen for the jobs you've had in the past. What feedback did you get? What did you consider your greatest strengths on the job? For now, just concentrate on those objective facts."

He agreed to do so, and he returned the next week with his lists. We studied them together, and I used them to help him stay connected to himself as an adult who was competent and talented at his work. The next step was to help Craig become connected to others. I reminded him that an adult is interdependent, not independent. Whom could he call that would understand his stress? What contacts did he have that could provide help?

Over the next few weeks, we created a plan for how Craig could stifle his frightened child and stay in an adult state while he looked for another job. It wasn't easy for him, and his interviews had plenty of ups and downs, but he managed it. Indeed, I've found that adults can deal with just about any crisis that comes their way. What they can't handle is the feeling that their weakness makes them so disgusting to others that they have to be alone in their crisis—that nobody else can stand them enough to share it. It's the isolation, not the crisis itself, that becomes intolerable.

POWERLESSNESS TRIGGERS SHAME

Most people have had the experience of feeling powerless at one time or another in their lives. Often, that feeling of powerlessness triggers the child's dependent reaction of shame. You know this is a child's reaction because adults never feel shame. An adult might feel regret, or longing, or disappointment, which are normal human reactions when your needs are not being met. For example, it was normal for Craig to feel anxious when he lost his job. But when that anxiety triggered shame, he was no longer in an adult state. In fact, it is impossible to exist securely in adulthood when you feel shame.

I realize that this is a controversial point of view, in light of current popular thinking—especially the work of John Bradshaw, whose writings and lectures about adult shame have been enthusiastically accepted by millions of people. Bradshaw teaches that all adults have shame, which he defines as "toxic" and "nontoxic." Toxic shame is the feeling your (abusive/dysfunctional) parents gave you that makes you feel horrible about yourself. Nontoxic shame is the inevitable way you feel when you do something wrong. According to Bradshaw, everyone experiences these feelings. Bradshaw started a process of helping people understand that dysfunctional parents leave their children a legacy of shame.

But I believe that *all* shame is toxic in adults, since it robs them of power. And it is inevitable in children, whether they grow up in "dysfunctional" homes or not, since shame is an outgrowth of dependency, and children are dependent. Of course, a child's feeling of shame can be worse if her parents abuse her and tell her she's no good. But anyone who has spent time around children knows that they are vulnerable to feeling embarrassed. That's because they have a keen sense of striving for mastery without the ability to do it. Think of the simple example of a child showing her mother a drawing she did at school. The mother thinks it's very cute, and she laughs. The child grabs it away in embarrassment and says accusingly, "You're laughing at me." Her mother protests. "No, I was laughing because I thought it was such a cute picture." But the child has no way of differentiating between her mother's delight and derision. She puts the picture away and doesn't show it to anyone else.

This is just the normal way a child responds. She lacks the perspective that would allow her to see her mother's laughter as loving. Of course, if her mother was consistently abusing her and telling her she was no good, it would increase her sense of shame. If her mother had said, "You call that a house? It's a terrible drawing!" she would immediately feel humiliated. But I am trying to make the point that children live in a state of dependency and react with shame, even when the adults around them are loving and supportive.

Bradshaw begins with the premise that most people grew up in dysfunctional families and the shame they feel is the outgrowth of negative experiences they had as children. I say if an adult feels shame, whether her family was dysfunctional or not, it's because she hasn't been trained to replace the child's dependency with the adult's interdependency.

In my work I've found that people always try to get better. It saps their life energy to live in a child's world. They want to live in a state of authentic adulthood. It's as necessary to human beings as breathing. I make the analogy of a plant reaching toward the light. If you take the plant and move it out of the sun, eventually you'll find that it twists around, instinctively searching for the light it needs and misses. People are like that, too. They always reach for the good. The problem isn't with their intentions, which are positive, but with the ways they have learned to fulfill those intentions.

THE CHILD FEELS HELPLESS

The reason dependency often leads to shame is because when a child doesn't get his needs met, he assumes it's because his needs are bad. Since he sees his parents as omnipotent, he believes that they don't give him what he wants or needs because they choose not to. And that must mean his needs are wrong. The child has no way to feel worthy unless the omnipotent adults constantly reinforce his worthiness.

I originally discovered this when I noticed that my patients always explained painful childhood experiences by assuming that they were to blame for the problems in their families. They would make statements like, "My parents fought all the time because we kids got on their nerves." Or, "Maybe my parents would have stayed together if I was good." Or, "My sister got sick right after I pushed her on the playground." In one poignant story, a man confessed that he'd spent most of his life thinking he'd caused his father's death because his father developed cancer following an episode when he'd lifted his son into the air and thrown out his back. "I was to blame for dad's bad back, and nobody ever told me that it didn't cause his cancer, so that's what I believed," the man told me. "My guilt was excruciating."

Children don't have the cognitive skills to understand that not everything that happens is directly related to them. They don't grasp, for example, that depression is an illness, or that their parents have problems that don't involve them. So when things go wrong, they feel responsible and ashamed. This conclusion is supported by the work of child psychologists who discovered, as the divorce rate increased, that children often believed they had done something to cause the divorce. They thought the pain they suffered was punishment for their wrongdoing. Because of emotional dyslexia, people keep making the same kinds of assumptions in adulthood—that everything is their fault.

Adults can feel helpless, too, when they're in a situation where someone else seems to have all of the power—especially when they don't have appropriate skills. Most people try to conquer the sense of helplessness by giving a form to it. It feels better if you think you can make yourself worthy by taking a specific action. So, you overwork, or overexercise, or overplease to reinforce your goodness. It's the longing to feel all right, to see oneself as basically lovable and good, that drives people to think their problems can be solved by being thinner or richer or nicer or more hardworking.

Since most children aren't taught to reinterpret their feelings of shame, they carry a core sense of unworthiness into adulthood. Even people who have undergone years of therapy, in order to feel better about themselves, often find that they can't hold onto the good feelings they've been able to develop when something negative happens. A lost love, a weight gain, an aging face, or a failure at work sparks the old feelings of humiliation, because they're still operating from the sense that to be grown up equals being perfect. The illusory but persistent feeling of wrongness is so painful that as the child matures he tries to find a way to rid himself of it. He looks at what the culture defines as good or bad and tries to become the "good" things to erase the shame.

Ironically, the greatest child's reactions are often found in the very people who seem on the surface to have the most power—the driven leader, the highly placed corporate executive, the beautiful woman who is desired by many men, or the Hollywood star. Their power is fragile, dependent on an ideal set of circumstances being in place.

Authentic adult power is not based on external circumstances. But most people let stressful circumstances trigger emotional dyslexia and they don't know how to transform their reactions. One of the best examples is the experience most people in our society have when they begin to grow older. Aging is normal and it is inevitable. You don't turn fifty because you did something bad. It's the way life works. Yet time and again, I work with people who are humiliated by the fact that they're growing older. For women, menopause has traditionally been the kiss of death. In a culture that glorifies youth and beauty, the older woman feels she no longer has a valid place. Lying about one's age is a sign of shame. The underlying feeling is, "I can't be acceptable as I am."

Growing older also stimulates the child's sense of vulnerability because it means a loss of the physical prowess and often mental power of youth. What do the elderly fear most? That they will become as helpless as children, that they will have needs they can no longer meet on their own, and that all of their past accomplishments will be erased.

Being sick tends to stimulate feelings of powerless— which trigger a child's reaction. I have a friend, Joanne, who had breast cancer, and she was unable to shake the despairing feeling that it was her fault. Furthermore, she felt guilty about how scared and unhappy she was; she thought she should be stronger. But she couldn't find her power.

After Joanne's cancer was diagnosed, I decided to help her engage her cognition to find more empowering responses. I made her a tape, and began by describing the predictable reactions that her disease was going to stimulate in her from the child's view. In this way, she could step outside her stress and become an observer:

"You're going to think the cancer is your fault and wonder what you might have done to prevent it.

"You're going to feel too needy with doctors and friends, and be embarrassed by that. You're going to worry that they'll get tired of your being sick and reject you.

"You're going to feel humiliated and inadequate, less than a 'real' woman, because you have lost a breast.

"You're going to be filled with envy for women who look good and have both of their breasts.

"Even though the loss of a breast is a catastrophic event, you aren't stuck with your feelings of shame and helplessness. When you find yourself feeling humiliated, jealous, or ashamed of your dependence on others, think of these responses as signals that you're heading into a child's state. Remind yourself:

" 'People get sick because they're human, and humans can't always avoid suffering, no matter how hard they try. You've always been very responsible about taking care of your health. It's not your fault that you got breast cancer.

" 'It's okay to feel weak when you're sick. You're lucky to have good friends and a good doctor who care about you and want to help you. You can ask them for help without feeling weak and dependent. In the past, you've been there for your friends when they were in need and you didn't think they were terrible people because they couldn't cope on their own. In fact, it made you feel good to know you were needed.

" 'You're married to a good man who is not disgusted because you have one breast. He hasn't rejected you. He loves you and only cares that you get better so you can continue your good life together.

" 'Of course, you get a pang of envy when you see women who have both of their breasts, but you know that your womanhood is not centered in your breast. You can still be feminine, attractive, and interesting to others.

" 'Sometimes the feeling of jealousy or panic are cues that you need to mourn. You're going to have down days when you need to release the stress. That's a natural part of healing, and it doesn't show weakness.' "

Joanne told me that she listened to the tape many times—especially when she started to slip into one of the child states. "It became my reality check," she said. "You weren't saying anything I didn't already know, but having the tape, which reinforced the positives over and over, made them more true for me." Eventually, Joanne stopped having to listen to the tape because she had internalized the message and was able to call it up on her own.

But it isn't just traumatic life events that stimulate feelings of powerlessness in people. One of my patients got angry whenever he felt any kind of weakness. When sales were off at his business, he was a stormy presence at home, criticizing his wife and children. When his wife had an asthma attack, he couldn't do anything to help her, so he shouted at her for not taking proper care of herself. Emotional dyslexia triggered the reaction, "It must be my fault. I have to fix it." When he couldn't, he grew angry.

You can stop feeling powerless if you maintain your adultness in spite of the circumstances. Adults understand at a fundamental level that their power doesn't depend on what they do for a living, how they look, how much money they have, or where they live. You can learn to internalize this truth and stop punishing yourself for things that aren't valid. And you can learn to see that behaviors in others that once seemed intimidating to you are merely signals that those people don't have the power they seem to have.

How can you tell the difference between authentic adult power and the false power that comes from the child? There are clues. The more you see the following behaviors, the greater are the indicators that people don't have real adult power:

- If they try to embarrass or demean you—even when they sugar-coat it. For example, "I'm only telling you this for your own good."
- If they give you information that can't really help you, but only makes you feel uncertain or embarrassed, such as, "Sue thinks you're a snob."
- If they pontificate or moralize, as if they know what's right, and call into question your values, morals, or intelligence, such as, "Only an idiot would say that."
- If they remind you about negative events and behaviors when you're feeling good, such as, "You look great now, but you know you always gain extra weight in the winter."
- If they exaggerate or lie to cover up the real circumstances—or if they rewrite history to make you look worse or themselves look better.
- If they always blame others and never examine themselves.
- If they are trapped in addictive or compulsive behaviors—not just drinking or overeating, but also overworking or being obsessed with accumulating power and money.

The most common triggers for helplessness seem to occur in the workplace. Not only is earning a living essential to our well-being but work is often used as a measure of who we are. People often complain to me that when things seem intolerable—when their real needs for sustenance as well as their dignity are challenged at every turn—they can't do a thing to stop themselves from acting like children. They feel impotent. That was Eileen's problem.

Eileen, a successful saleswoman for a major magazine,

was having a terrible time with her boss. In the six months since he had been promoted to his position, he had made her life miserable. She would have quit her job if she'd been able to find anything comparable. But after months of suffering at the hands of this irrational man, and failing to find another job that was as good, she came to me to see if I could help her.

"He despises me," she said. "The better I do, the worse he gets." She said that every time she made a new commission, her boss reacted negatively. "He puts me down in meetings; he undermines my authority with the people I supervise. Now he's even started cutting my percentages on commissions, so I make less money," she said. "It's so crazy. It makes no sense. He should want me to do well, since it reflects on him. But it's like he's trying to destroy me. He's made it impossible for me to do my job. And it's not as if I can leave. I've put out some discreet feelers, and there are no jobs at my level with the kind of compensation I'm getting. I'd have to take a 50 percent pay cut. So I feel completely stuck in this nightmare."

As Eileen described her boss's behavior, it became clear to me that he was very threatened by her success. His actions were an attempt to gain the upper hand so that her looking good wouldn't make him look bad. In Eileen's eyes, he had a lot of power, and indeed, he did have a certain amount of objective power that could not be disputed. He could cut Eileen's commissions and influence her position in the company. But on a fundamental level, this man was not operating as a person who was powerful. He was behaving like a child whose fear of looking bad is so great that he attacks without apparent cause—the schoolyard bully who terrorizes the smaller kids.

I was intent on helping Eileen shift her perspective on this man so she would feel less victimized by him—to find a way to regain her power in a situation where she felt powerless. I began by helping her engage her cognitive brain to clarify her goal. She had a dilemma: She didn't want to get a different job, so she had to find a way to get power in her current position.

I asked Eileen why she thought her boss acted that way. She was uncertain. "Maybe I'm too aggressive. I push hard to get what I want."

"You sell advertising space," I reminded her. "Don't you have to be aggressive to do a good job?"

"Yes. But still, maybe if I toned it down a little, I'd get along better with my boss."

"Are you the only person in the office that he treats this way?"

"It's worse with me, because he's my direct supervisor, but he's not the most pleasant guy. In meetings, if anyone else has an idea, he's always got a list of reasons why it won't work. And he's always looking for someone to blame if anything goes wrong. He yells at his secretary a lot. That kind of thing."

"So, it's not just about you," I said. "It's very different if you think he's behaving this way as a reaction to something you're doing than if you believe his behavior stems from something inside him."

Eileen looked uncertain. "I can see that, but the bottom line is still the same. He's the boss and he can do anything he wants. He has the full support of our top management. He's on the fast track, and he's always been very successful at every job the agency has given him. In spite of the way he's treating me, he's actually a pretty talented guy."

I wanted to help Eileen see her boss in a different light. "He has certain kinds of power," I told her. "But his behavior toward you isn't a sign of power. Think about it. Can you imagine yourself treating people in the way he's treated you if you were feeling secure and good about yourself?"

She looked at me with new interest. "No. Usually when I'm feeling great I'm more generous and open with people."

"Right. Powerful, confident people don't have to demean others. When your boss puts you down or reduces your commissions, he's acting like a vengeful, scared child. At his core, he feels bad about himself."

"So, I'm supposed to be understanding?" Eileen asked sarcastically. "Poor guy, he's insecure, so it's okay if he walks all over me?"

"No," I laughed. "That's not the point. It's just that the more you understand where he's coming from, and what makes him tick, the more control you'll feel when you're confronted by his behavior. The point is, you can use this knowledge to maneuver in your job. This is really about choice—the ways you have of making your goal work. Just because a man has been successful in his career doesn't mean he feels secure and full of self-worth. Often, the reverse is true. Your boss is treating you this way because he's afraid of being humiliated. He expects humiliation. So he's going to get to you before you have a chance to get to him." I could see Eileen was puzzled. "Maybe this image will help. Consider that your boss is standing in front of a mirror and speaking to himself, instead of to you or one of the other people in the office. Tell me something he typically says."

"He can really put people down," Eileen said thoughtfully. "Not just me. The other day, he told one of the young guys in our department, 'How did they ever let you out of school? You're hopeless.' "

"Okay. He's facing himself in a mirror and saying, 'How did they ever let you out of school? You're hopeless.' His harsh judgements of others are really based on his own fear of screwing up—his desperation that he might get discovered as an imposter and be humiliated. If you imagine that every cutting remark he makes is self-directed, you'll have a much more accurate sense of what he's really feeling."

Eileen leaned back against the cushions of the sofa, looking intrigued and baffled. "You're asking me to make a big shift in thinking," she said. "It has never occurred to me that my boss behaves the way he does to hide his own insecurities. He's always seemed so powerful."

It wasn't so obvious, especially to Eileen who had to suffer daily torment from this man, that he was exhibiting all the signs of someone who was afraid. He could not applaud Eileen for her work because he was jealous. When something went wrong, he immediately looked for someone to blame, just to make sure the finger wasn't pointed in his direction. When people suggested new ideas in meetings, he shot them down—playing it safe so he wouldn't risk failure.

My goal was to give Eileen a strategy that would allow her to regain her own sense of power by not blaming herself for her boss's behavior. Viewing him as a frightened child helped her do this. Then the issue was, how to disarm the man and make him less of an impediment to her work. We talked about it over the next several weeks and finally devised a strategy. Eileen finally acknowledged that confrontation was the worst possible response to someone who felt threatened. It would only make matters worse.

Since her boss was putting her down because he was afraid of getting put down himself, we decided to short-circuit the process by building him up—in other words, giving him a different result than the one he expected. Every time her boss implemented something positive, suggested a good idea, or had a success, Eileen made sure to acknowledge it, verbally or in a memo. She used a form of strategic communication to keep him from anticipating humiliation so he didn't have to put her down first. In effect, she conditioned him not to see her as a threat.

Over time, Eileen's boss came to see her more as an ally than a threat. It still wasn't a perfect environment, but at least he stopped cutting her commissions and undermining her in front of the staff. Most important, Eileen felt better about herself. She learned that she could change a situation that wasn't working. In the child's state, she had felt impotent. As an adult, she felt powerful.

Authentic adult power gives you an impact in the world where before you felt impotent. This power is available to every adult. It comes with skills, not with external trappings. The following lesson will help you practice being powerful by avoiding the triggers that make you feel weak.

Adult Skill: Find Your Power When It Seems You Have None

Our most important ego need after survival is to feel that our core beings are worthy. That sense of worthiness is the door to personal power. Powerful people know that they have the ability to make an impact on the world. They hold a positive sense of themselves that keeps them feeling worthy and strong. This lesson will help you to hold onto your positive self to avoid acting from weakness, even in difficult situations. There are three steps to this lesson:

1. *Stop* and reconnect with your power.
2. *Review* the ways true power is manifested.
3. *Reshape* yourself as a powerful problem solver.

STEP 1: Stop and reconnect with your power.

You don't want to be impotent in life. You're not acting in ways to deliberately sabotage your chances. But sometimes feelings of impotence overwhelm you. When that happens, you can't seem to get a grip on your power. Maybe you begin acting ineffectively and even you can't understand why. Before you let your self-esteem spiral downward, stop and give yourself an opportunity to reconnect with your power.

Remember the "of course" exercise you learned in Lesson Three? That can be applied as a helpful tool in recognizing your power. To demonstrate, here's the way I used it with Larry, a man who came to see me because he was having trouble functioning at work. His original explanation was, "I guess I'm just lazy."

"How so?" I asked.

"One of my jobs is to write reports for top management, and I just can't seem to get them done," he said. "I procrastinate and avoid doing them. Lately, I've been oversleeping and getting to work late."

Was Larry really lazy? My first task was to help him describe his problem without being judgmental—to use words other than a negative flag word like *lazy* to describe his behavior. I did this by asking him to put himself in the role of his best friend, using the "of course" response.

"You've just told him about your struggle getting the reports done. What does he say?"

Larry thought about it for a moment, and then his face broke into a smile. "He says, 'Of course, you don't want to do those reports. They're just bureaucratic busy work, and they're boring. Your talents are much more creative.' "

As he repeated his friend's imagined response, Larry visibly relaxed. He was beginning to move away from self-blame and view his problem in another light.

Next, I asked Larry to choose someone he respected—a mentor—and imagine telling that person his story. Larry chose a coach from his high school days, a man he had always admired.

"What does the coach say?" I asked.

"He says, 'Oh, the people in the corporate office only care about the bottom line. They're just number crunchers. That's what these reports are all about. I don't blame you for being bored.' "

After Larry "listened" to the reactions of his friend and mentor, I asked him to redefine his problem. He discarded the negative word *lazy*. "I'm not lazy," he said with relief. "The work doesn't challenge me."

Larry's discovery didn't stop there, because discarding

negative self-definitions isn't about making excuses for inappropriate behavior. Some popular psychological approaches stop at this point. They don't lead to a change in behavior, but to a justification that allows the negative behavior to continue. The truth is, no matter how many times you repeat the mantra that you're "okay," if your behavior is causing you problems, you're going to stop believing it. The "of course" response can be a prelude to change. This exercise places you in a position to review your options without shame getting in the way.

Over a period of weeks, I helped Larry consider how he might change his situation, now that he understood the problem wasn't simply his "laziness." He began by enrolling in a night course to explore his interest in computers. Later, he changed jobs and became a troubleshooter for a computer service. He called to tell me how much he loved his new line of work. "I'm really charged up," he said happily. "I love what I'm doing, and I don't have a problem with oversleeping anymore." He laughed. "In fact, I'm up with the birds."

Using Larry's experience as a guide, focus on your own situation, and ask yourself questions:

1. Is there an area of your life where you lack control or feel weak? Your experience might be related to job, health, money, community, or a personal relationship.
2. What do you say to yourself about your weakness? For example:

"I'm just a cog in a wheel."
"I don't have any money. I'm a loser."

Notice if you're using descriptions that reinforce a negative position. Write down an adult replacement response. For example:

"I'm not the boss, but I can control the quality of my work and find satisfaction in a job well done."

"I'd feel more comfortable if I had more money, but money is not the sole indicator of my worth. If my problem is needing more money, I can problem solve ways to earn it."

The key is to describe your problem in a way that does not challenge your core worthiness. Finding the positive intent always leads to action. It opens the doors to your options and gives you a way to problem solve.

STEP 2: **Review the ways true power is manifested.**

Learn to recognize the difference between real power that comes from authentic adulthood, and the mask of power that covers up the child's feelings of weakness.

During the course of a week, make a note of every time you see someone being powerful. This can be a person in your own life, a political leader, or even someone in a movie or a book. Find as many examples as you can.

At the end of the week, consider your examples and determine if each person's power came from the adult or the child. Use the E.D. Index to look for clues:

Was the "powerful" person

- afraid of looking bad? (shame)
- blaming someone else? (victimization)
- making excuses? (impotence)
- being self-important? (egocentricity)
- demanding instant attention? (impatience)
- proposing magical solutions? (fantasy)
- refusing to negotiate? (rigidity)
- comparing himself to others? (jealousy)
- causing upset in those around her? (melodrama)

Or, was the "powerful" person

- being dignified? (worthiness)
- accepting responsibility? (freedom)
- offering real solutions? (power)
- considering others' needs? (empathy)
- looking at the long term? (patience)
- making tough decisions? (reality)
- looking at the options? (flexibility)
- being self-expressive? (fulfillment)
- motivating others by example? (peace)

Once you become accustomed to observing others through the screen of the E.D. Index, you'll become accomplished at recognizing when people have authentic adult power, and when their actions are motivated by a child's needs. You can then apply the lesson in your own life.

Step 3: Reshape yourself as a powerful problem solver.

You are the choreographer of your own life, and no one can take that away from you. But E.D. triggers a feeling of helplessness. You feel stuck, trapped, unable to get out of the hole that is making you uncomfortable. Once you engage your cognitive brain, solutions become possible. Even when you are in a situation that you can't change, relating to it from a child's state will make you weak. Adults have two options: to make a change or to change their relationship to a situation. Either response is empowering.

Step away from your problem and view it as if you were an outside observer. Ask yourself these questions:

1. What is my goal?

Example:

"To be fulfilled in my work."
"To increase my income."
"To find a job that will use my creativity."

2. List the impediments to your goal. Concentrate on using adult language from the E.D. Index. That is, stay away from the language of impotence, jealousy, rigidity, and so forth. For example:

Child	*Adult*
"The job market is closed tight. There are no good jobs in my field."	"This is a tough market, so I have to be more creative than ever."

3. Consider your options. An adult always has options. For example, if you are looking for a better job, examine all the possibilities: Who can you talk to? What contacts can you use? What can you do to get your foot in the door? What compromises are you willing to make?

Maybe your options for action are limited, but you can still help your situation by seeking support from others—even if that means simply talking to a friend to remind you of your goodness.

Adult power comes from interdependency. Almost any crisis can be handled if you don't feel isolated and unworthy. If you try to solve all of your problems alone, you're falling into the child's view that grown-ups are supposed to be omnipotent. Your power comes from engaging fully in the human community, not going it alone.

CHAPTER 10

Can You Be a Grown-up in Every Situation?

- Do your problems feel overwhelming at times?
- Is there any way to be an adult in this period of high unemployment, social collapse, AIDS?
- Is it sometimes just too hard to be a grown-up?

I have had people stand up in my workshops, after listening to everything I've said, and cry out in anguish and despair: "How can I keep it together? My husband's out of work. We're going to lose everything." Or, "My son is sick. He might die. There's no way to make it better." Once a woman responded to another person in a workshop with, "I wish I had your problems! They seem easy compared to caring for a mother with Alzheimer's."

It's true that sometimes the overwhelming anxieties of life throw you a curve so big that it knocks the wind out of you. You lose your job, get sick, a loved one dies, your child gets arrested for stealing, or a hurricane destroys your home. How can you be expected to be an adult when your world crumbles?

Part of the problem of living in an emotionally dyslexic society is that people are not taught the skills they need to handle life's inevitable adult crises. So, when real problems show up, they seem too huge to withstand. People panic. They avoid issues and look the other way—like the woman who refuses to get a breast biopsy when she finds a lump. Or the couple who decides that not answering the phone is the best response to bill collectors. Sometimes we become magical thinkers, hoping that if we don't talk about illness, death, or the process of aging, they will elude us. Remember, it wasn't so long ago that the word *cancer* carried with it the cachet of shame.

Of course, neither avoidance nor magic saves people from the realities of life. And when they're finally up against the wall, they wail, "How could this happen to me? It wasn't supposed to be this way!"

When you're not prepared for them, the natural processes of life and death come as a tremendous shock to you. Not only are you stressed by the events themselves but you have the added burden of lugging around the child's shame, guilt, jealousy, and helplessness. Then, life's stresses feel like punishment because your child's voice says that bad things don't happen to people who have their lives "together."

You can't live like an adult and also feel that you're to blame for everything that happens to you—up to and including death.

My answer to those who wonder how it is possible to maintain adult skills when the worst happens is this: You can respond to a terrible crisis as a child, without any tools at all for coping. Or you can respond as an adult and use the resources you have to ease the suffering.

I think that sometimes people get confused about what adult behavior is. Let me reiterate what it is not:

Being an adult does not mean that you're in perfect control. The predictable life crises of sickness, death, financial woes, and sometimes the destruction of dreams happen to human beings. You may be a well-functioning adult, but you're not invincible. Remember, the idea that adults are omnipotent comes from the child's state.

Being an adult does not mean being a stoic. When there's real danger in your life, you respond to it. Your emotions intensify. You feel legitimate grief, fear, anger, or confusion. Awareness of mortality causes legitimate existential anxiety in adults.

Being an adult does not even guarantee that you're not going to have childlike responses triggered when something bad happens to you.

This approach is not a magical solution to every problem. But if you have adult skills, you'll find that your responses to real crises are more manageable, and you have more power to face them. You see, childlike reactions only add layers of trauma to already traumatic situations. Not only do you feel the sadness, fear, or confusion that is relevant to the crisis but you are also burdened by fears that are inappropriate and only make things worse. You are trying to solve big problems with small resources. I believe that when you live at your best, as an adult, you can cope with the existential anxiety that is inevitable because suffering is a part of living.

YOU'RE ONLY HUMAN

Superheroes belong in the realm of fantasy. Real life is rugged and often unpredictable. You may feel stunned by grief or pain, and wonder why the hand of fate dealt you such a lousy card, but the truth is, there's no one alive who hasn't experienced sickness, the death of loved ones, or other moments of pain and vulnerability. These events can tear you apart, but they're not really extraordinary. Everyone dies. Everyone is vulnerable. It's the human state.

I think of Joyce, the woman who said it to me with burning anguish, "Look at me. I'm getting old. I'm fifty. How did this happen?" Joyce was experiencing the feeling of having sleep-walked through her life. Her fear of aging and mortality was based on her despair at never being fully alive. She said, "I feel like I went to sleep at twenty-five and woke up at fifty." She was in mourning for all those lost years.

Turning fifty put a stamp on Joyce's sense of failure. Instead of feeling that she was experiencing a rite of passage that showed she had arrived, she felt defeated because she had never learned the skills she needed to have a satisfying adult life. Her age didn't bother her as much as her deep sense that she wasn't having the quality of life appropriate to her age. Her marriage had failed, and after many years of living alone, she was frightened that she'd grow old and never have what she wanted. Already, some of her goals—like having children—were beyond her reach. And she was so intimidated by the youth culture all around her that she said she felt like a dinosaur.

They didn't know that what they needed were the adult skills that would have enabled them to live with pleasure, satisfaction, and mastery. Instead, they focused on the external qualities of a youth culture.

My work with Joyce centered on her learning the skills to accept what had happened in the past without letting it paralyze her future, and to see that people can age gracefully if they mature as they age. I suggested replacement adult responses for the shame she felt over her failed marriage and her feelings of jealousy toward women who had husbands and children. "It's understandable and appropriate to feel regret for the things that never were," I said. "Everyone has regrets and disappointments. If you can let yourself experience your regret, you'll find that it doesn't send you into a helpless state; it doesn't denigrate you. It's simply there—an authentic emotion. And on the other side of regret is the energy to make choices for the future because you're not bogged down by shame."

Of course, at the bottom of fear of aging is the fear of death, which can be viewed as the ultimate loss of control, and also the most predictable event of all. It happens to everyone. But if you've never come to an understanding that adults are not invincible, your expectations of yourself and others are beyond reality.

Living in a world without authentic adult role models leaves an emptiness we're always trying to fill. In our society, we constantly turn ordinary human beings into heroes, then are disappointed when they fail to live up to our expectations. Read the newspaper or listen to the TV news reports any day of the week and you'll find a dozen examples of hero worship gone awry. If we assign superhuman qualities to our leaders, and believe they always know exactly what to do in every situation (there's no doubt or ambivalence in their lives!), then we are naturally disappointed when they screw up. We get angry when our heroes fail us because we're looking for role models of power based on our childlike perceptions.

If we think there is a man or woman alive who will not face death, who somehow "has it all," we are shocked when their humanity is revealed. An authentic adult is aware of his humanity and the humanity of others.

REACHING FOR THE LIGHT

Sometimes life does seem too much to bear, and we are made deeply aware of our human frailty. Today, we are living in a time when there is an epidemic of depression. It feels like the world is exploding in hatred, disease, and malaise—problems too great for any human to solve. On a personal level, most of us have daily brushes with despair. We see it on the streets of our cities, in the hopeless eyes of the friend who has AIDS, in the helplessness of the elderly parent who has become like our child, in the business that announces yet another series of layoffs.

Most people feel too stressed and isolated. The families and communities that once gave comfort and support in times of crisis have long since dissolved. The rituals that once brought people together in times of happiness and sorrow have been discarded, and they haven't been replaced. People live in separation and confusion, and they think they have to bear the full weight of life all alone.

No one wants to live in misery, fear, and hopelessness. Remember the story of the plant that always sought out the light, even if it had to twist its entire body to find it? We are like that plant, always searching for the light, always looking for ways to make our lives have meaning and purpose.

But if you feel deeply wounded and spiritually empty, and the solutions you've sought have not provided relief, where do you turn for solace? How do you keep reaching for the light when it has become so elusive?

People are initially skeptical when I tell them that transforming their emotional dyslexia into adult skills will make their lives work better. They fear it is one more theory designed to disappoint them, and I can certainly understand their skepticism. You can't trust any process unless you feel better when you try it. But the ability to be a powerful adult exists within you. But the power of adulthood rests in you, not in an external force.

If you remove E.D., you'll attract love because you'll be able to feel love yourself.

If you remove E.D., you'll find power because you'll accept the ambiguities and imperfections of the world.

If you remove E.D., you'll know spirituality because you'll embrace life as an adult.

And if you remove E.D., you'll find abiding peace because you'll put your "child" to rest, and approach yourself as a real, worthy, powerful adult.

INDEX